The Children's Book of Comic Verse

The Children's Book of

COMIC VERSE

Chosen by Christopher Logue
Illustrated by Bill Tidy

Suitable for:
The Worst Girl of the Year and/or The Thickest Boy Ever; lazy
children; children who answer back; children who are late
for meals and who leave half their food; children who cannot
stand animals, family holidays, 'sharing', and housework;
children who pick their noses, read under the blankets,
steal from sweet-shops, tell lies, bang doors, never
clean their shoes and always dirty their clothes;
sulky children; children with very loud voices;
children who refuse to 'speak up'; children who
think about nothing except knickers, guns,
make-up, parties, telephone-calls, and
leaving school; children who hate sports
and all forms of physical exercise;
very small children who are always being stepped on;
very large children
who are always in the way;
middle-sized children;
children who dislike children;
children who think that
The Rhyme of The Ancient Mariner is about Noah,
and that *metre* is short for *gasmeter*;
children who never read anything
(except TV programmes).

B. T. Batsford Ltd, London

To
Fred Ingrams
and
Poppy Luard

The Monarch wrote to the Captain of the Host:
'If you, Sir, would be savèd,
Put Uriah in the thickest of the fight,
Yours in haste, King David.'

First published 1979
Selection copyright Christopher Logue 1979
Illustration copyright Bill Tidy 1979
Filmset in Sabon by Keyspools Ltd, Golborne, Lancashire
Printed and bound in Great Britain by
Butler & Tanner Ltd, Frome
for The Publisher, B. T. Batsford Ltd,
4 Fitzhardinge Street, London, W1H 0AH
ISBN 0 7134 1528 2

Contents

To the Reader

Luckily for us both there is little to be said about the verses that follow. They are meant to make you laugh; if they do not, too bad for their authors, for me – and for you.

Let me explain the meaning of the word *irony*. Irony is a way of using words to say the opposite of what they mean:

The gentleman who had the good fortune to teach me Poetry at school was called Mr Witt. 'Stiffy' Witt to us, because he broke his neck by tripping over Shakespeare's gravestone during a country ramble and could thereafter neither shake nor nod his head.

Although I did everything I could to make Mr Witt's lessons interesting, he took a dislike to my voice, which, I must admit, even my mother thought was rather loud for a boy of twelve.

So when (FOR NO REASON WHATSOEVER) Mr Witt wished to put me in my place, he would say, 'Logue, stand up and recite *The Charge of the Light Brigade* – and do not whisper.' His kindly recommendation always drew a laugh from the wittiest boys in the class.

In fact, Mr Witt was a good, patient man, who taught at least one of his pupils to love Poetry; and I was, probably, a pest.

Christopher Logue

The Showman's Song

If you step into my show, Sir,
I've no end of things you'll know, Sir,
I've a rabbit that wears snow-shoes with a house in Mozambique;
I've a team of skating poodles,
I've a goldfish that cooks noodles,
And a chicken that can see into the middle of next week.

I've a cockle that drinks gum, Sir,
And a cow that beats the drum, Sir,
While the vulture and the tadpole and the lion sing a glee;
Plus an eel that is so long, Sir,
He could scoff the Loch Ness Monster;
I've a camel with a weakness for a winkle with his tea.

I've a cricketing canary,
And an earwig known as Mary;
I've a melancholy lizard who is often on TV;
While my ostrich and my gurnet
Spend their money (when they earn it)
On *The Times* and *Gardener's Weekly* – which they always lend
to me.

Heed my brace of surfing eagles,
Hear my pack of talking beagles,
Meet my glamorous, adaptable, creative Major Frog
Who composed a five act drama –
While his friend, the mountain llama,
With a quill from Mr Porcupine knocked off the epilogue.

O, the walrus keen on waltzing,
And the crocodiles who all sing
God Save The Queen and *Tosca*, will delight you in my tent;
All in all you'll love the show, Sir,
You will never wish to go, Sir,
O, I promise you will not regret the penny you have spent.

adapted from J. H. Byron

To The Moon

O Moon! when I look on your beautiful face
Careering along through the darkness of space,
The thought has quite frequently come to my mind
If ever I'll gaze on your lovely behind.

Anonymous

Hokee Pokee

Hokee Pokee!
Hankee Pankee!
I'm the Queen of Swinkee Swankee!
And I'm pretty well
I thankee.

Charles Henry Ross

The Cares of a Caretaker

A nice old lady by the sea
    Was neat as she was plain,
And every time the tide came in
    She swept it back again.

And when the sea untidy grew
    And waves began to beat,
She took her little garden rake
    And raked it smooth and neat.

She ran a carpet-sweeper up
    And down the pebbly sand.
She said, 'This is the only way
    To keep it clean – good land!'

And when the gulls came strolling by,
    She drove them shrilly back,
Remarking that it spoiled the beach,
    'The way them birds do track.'

She fed the catfish clotted cream
    And taught it how to purr –
And were a catfish so endowed
    She would have stroked its fur.

She stopped the little sea-urchins
    That travelled by in pairs,
And washed their dirty faces clean
    And combed their little hairs.

She spread white napkins on the surf
  With which she fumed and fussed.
'When it ain't covered up,' she said,
  'It gits all over dust.'

She didn't like to see the ships
  With all the waves act free,
And so she got a painted sign
  Which read: *Keep off the Sea.*

But dust and splutter as she might,
  Her work was sadly vain;
However oft she swept the beach,
  The tides came in again.

And she was sometimes wan and worn
  When she retired to bed –
'A woman's work ain't never done,'
  That nice old lady said.

Wallace Irwin

The Pickle

There was a little pickle and he hadn't any name –
In this respect, I'm just informed, all pickles are the same.
A large policeman came along, a-swinging of his club,
And took that little pickle up and put him in a tub.

Charles Edward Carryl

Doctor Foster

Doctor Foster went to Gloucester
  In a shower of rain;
He stepped in a puddle, up to his middle,
  And never went there again.

Anonymous

The Cow

I'm sure you all have seen a Cow,
   But, just in case you've not,
An artist, from his lofty mind,
Has drawn one, which I think you'll find
   To be quite as it ought.

You cannot thank the Cow enough
   For all the milk you drink:
That all this fluid fresh and blue
Comes straight from Cows to nourish you
   Is wonderful to think.

Yet, when we find thermometers
   At '90 in the shade,'
How nice 'twould be if Cows would see
Their way to act obligingly –
   And give us Lemonade.

John Joy Bell

Tommy Jones – The Educated Pug

I had an educated pug,
  His name was Tommy Jones;
He lived upon the parlor rug
  Exclusively on bones.

And if, in a secluded room,
  I hid one on a shelf,
It disappeared; so I presume
  He used to help himself.

He had an entertaining trick
  Of feigning he was dead;
Then, with a reassuring kick,
  Would stand upon his head.

I could not take the proper change,
  And go to buy him shoes,
But he would sit upon the range
  And read the latest news.

And when I ventured out, one day,
  To order him a coat,
I found him, in his artless way,
  Careering on a goat.

I could not go to look at hats
  But that, with childish glee,
He'd ask in all the neighbors' cats
  To join him at his tea.

And when I went to pay a bill
  (I think it was for tripe),
He made himself extremely ill
  By smoking uncle's pipe.

                Charles Edward Carryl

The Village Burglar

Under the spreading gooseberry bush
   The village burglar lies;
The burglar is a hairy man
   With whiskers round his eyes.

He goes to church on Sundays;
   He hears the Parson shout;
He puts a penny in the plate
   And takes a shilling out.

Anonymous

My Aunt

My aunt she died a month ago
   And left me all her riches –
A feather-bed, a wooden leg,
   And a pair of calico britches.
A coffee-pot without a spout,
   A mug without a handle,
A 'baccy box without a lid,
   And half a farthing candle.

Anonymous

The Happy Hedgehog

The happiness of hedgehogs
   Lies in complete repose.
They spend the months of winter
   In a long delicious doze;
And if they note the time at all
   They think 'How fast it goes!'

E. V. Rieu

Nothing To Do ?

Nothing to do ?
Nothing to do ?
Put some mustard in your shoe,
Fill your pockets full of soot,
Drive a nail into your foot,
Put some sugar in your hair,
Place your toys upon the stair,
Smear some jelly on the latch,
Eat some mud and strike a match,
Draw a picture on the wall,
Roll some marbles down the hall,
Pour some ink in daddy's cap –
    Now go upstairs and take a nap.

Shelley Silverstein

Amelia

Amelia mixed the mustard,
    She mixed it good and thick;
She put it in the custard
    And made her Mother sick,
And showing satisfaction
    By many a loud hurrah,
'Observe,' she said 'the action
    Of mustard on Mamma.'

A. E. Housman

As I Was Going Out One Day

As I was going out one day
My head fell off and rolled away.
But when I saw that it was gone,
I picked it up and put it on.

And when I got into the street
A fellow cried: 'Look at your feet!'
I looked at them and sadly said:
'I've left them both asleep in bed!'

Anonymous

My Lord Tomnoddy

My Lord Tomnoddy's the son of an Earl,
His hair is straight, but his whiskers curl;
His Lordship's forehead is far from wide,
But there's plenty of room for the brains inside.
He writes his name with indifferent ease,
He's rather uncertain about the 'd's,' –
But what does it matter, if three or one,
To the Earl of Fitzdotterel's eldest son?

My Lord Tomnoddy to college went,
Much time he lost, much money he spent;
Rules, and windows, and heads, he broke –
Authorities wink'd – young men will joke!
He never peep'd inside of a book –
In two years' time a degree he took;
And the newspapers vaunted the honours won
By the Earl of Fitzdotterel's eldest son.

My Lord Tomnoddy came out in the world,
Waists were tighten'd, and ringlets curl'd.
Virgins languish'd, and matrons smil'd –
'Tis true, his Lordship is rather wild;
In very queer places he spends his life;
There's talk of some children, by nobody's wife –
But we mustn't look close into what is done
By the Earl of Fitzdotterel's eldest son.

My Lord Tomnoddy must settle down –
There's a vacant seat in the family town!
('Tis time he should sow his eccentric oats) –
He hasn't the wit to apply for votes:
He cannot e'en learn his election speech,
Three phrases he speaks – a mistake in each!
And then breaks down – but the borough is won
For the Earl of Fitzdotterel's eldest son.

My Lord Tomnoddy prefers the Guards,
(The House is a bore) so! – it's on the cards!
My Lord's a Lieutenant at twenty-three,
A Captain at twenty-six is he –

He never drew sword, except on drill;
The tricks of parade he has learnt but ill –
A full-blown Colonel at thirty-one
Is the Earl of Fitzdotterel's eldest son!

My Lord Tomnoddy is thirty-four;
The Earl can last but a few years more.
My Lord in the Peers will take his place:
Her Majesty's councils his words will grace.
Office he'll hold, and patronage sway;
Fortunes and lives he will vote away –
And what are his qualifications ? – ONE!
He's the Earl of Fitzdotterel's eldest son!

Robert Barnabas Brough

The Dumps

We're all in the dumps,
For diamonds are trumps;
The kittens are gone to St. Paul's!
The babies are bit,
The moon's in a fit,
And the houses are built without walls.

Anonymous

Madrid

There was an old man of Madrid,
Who ate sixty-five eggs for a quid.
        When they asked, 'Are you faint ?'
        He replied, 'No, I ain't,
But I don't feel as well as I did.'

Anonymous

Peas

I eat my peas with honey,
I've done it all my life;
It makes the peas taste funny,
But it keeps them on the knife.

Anonymous

SCHOOL DINNERS

Toast

I had never had a piece of toast
Particularly long and wide,
But fell upon the sanded floor,
And always on the buttered side.

James Payn

Little Clotilda

Little Clotilda,
Well and hearty,
Thought she'd like
To give a party.
But as her friends
Were shy and wary,
Nobody came
But her own canary.

Anonymous

There Once was a King

There once was a King did a very sad thing –
He nipped all the buds off the flowers in spring.
When the thistles and weeds heard tell of his deeds,
They shook their old heads till they shook out their seeds,
Then they rose by the score, and choked up his door,
So he couldn't get out to do harm any more.
There, a lesson to teach, they left him to screech,
Whilst the flowers grew gaily just out of his reach.

Charles Henry Ross

Posers

Supposing you had 6 baboons,
    And made them dance a dozen jigs,
How many pairs of pantaloons
    Would equal 50 sucking-pigs ?

If every house had 7 roofs,
    And every roof 1,000 tiles,
How much is worn off horses' hoofs
    In trotting 20,000 miles ?

If 60 stockings made a pair,
    And all our hats were worn in twos,
How many braces should we wear,
    Including slippers, boots, and shoes ?

If 20 kittens made a pie
    Of half a 100 mouses' tails,
How far is Rome from Peckham Rye
    Before the equinoctial gales ?

If 40 snails could crawl a mile
    In $\frac{1}{2}$ the time it takes to wink,
How many pills would cure the bile ? –
    Please work it out in pen and ink.

If 7 double-barrell'd guns
    Kill'd 80 rabbits in an hour,
How many pounds of hot-cross-buns
    Could Jumbo in a day devour ?

If every dog had 50 barks,
    And every bark 11 bites,
How many children's Noah's Arks
    Would equal 2 electric lights ?

If 30 chimney-pots of ale,
    And $\frac{1}{2}$ a looking-glass of wine,
Were all reduced to smallest scale,
    What is it multiplied by 9 ?

If 7 senses are confused
    By whales 600 acres long,
Why shouldn't people be amused
    At this my idiotic song ?

X. Parke

A Beastly Questionnaire

Have Angleworms attractive homes ?
  Do Bumblebees have brains ?
Do Caterpillars carry combs ?
  Do Dodos dote on drains ?
Can Eels elude elastic earls ?
  Do Flatfish fish for flats ?
Are Grigs agreeable to girls ?
  Do Hares have hunting-hats ?
Do Ices make an Ibex ill ?
  Do Jackdaws jug their jam ?
Do Kites kiss all the kids they kill ?
  Do Llamas live on lamb ?
Will Moles molest a mounted mink ?
  Do Newts deny the news ?
Are Oysters boisterous when they drink ?
  Do Parrots prowl in pews ?
Do Quakers get their quills from Quails ?
  Do Rabbits rob on roads ?
Are Snakes supposed to sneer at snails ?
  Do Tortoises tease toads ?
Can Unicorns perform on horns ?
  Do Vipers value veal ?
Do Weasels weep when fast asleep ?
  Can Xylophagans squeal ?
Do Yaks in packs invite attacks ?
  Are Zebras full of zeal ?

Charles Edward Carryl

Tutor

A tutor who taught on the flute
Tried to teach two young tooters to toot.
    Said the two to the tutor,
    'Is it harder to toot, or
To tutor two tooters to toot ?'

Anonymous

Hospitality

We had Kenneth and Mary for Easter,
  And Kate and the twins came in May.
Then Louise for a week, with her bad-tempered Peke,
  And it poured every day of their stay.

Then Joanna and Dick came for Whitsun
  And a student from France in July.
And every week-end brings some dear old friend,
  Who pops in as he's passing by.

There were Charles, Jean and Roger in August,
  Then next we had Betty and John,
And old Uncle Paul, whose possessions were all
  Left in cupboards for me to send on.

I cooked and I fed and sight-showed them,
  And I learnt this the hard, hard way,
It's an odd sort of boast – get a name as a host
  And no one will ask *you* to stay.

Anne Haward

I Said

I said, 'This horse, sir, will you shoe?'
  And soon the horse was shod.
I said, 'This deed, sir, will you do?'
  And soon the deed was dod!

I said, 'This stick, sir, will you break?'
  At once the stick he broke.
I said, 'This coat, sir, will you make?'
  And soon the coat he moke!

Anonymous

NO!

No sun – no moon!
No morn – no noon –
No dawn – no dusk – no proper time of day –
No sky – no earthly view –
No distance looking blue –
No road – no street – no 't'other side the way' –
No end to any Row –
No indications where the Crescents go –
No top to any steeple –
No recognitions of familiar people –
No courtesies for showing 'em –
No knowing 'em!
No travelling at all – no locomotion,
No inkling of the way – no notion –
'No go' – by land or ocean –
No mail – no post –
No news from any foreign coast –
No park – no ring – no afternoon gentility –
No company – no nobility –
No warmth, no cheerfulness, no healthful ease,
No comfortable feel in any member –
No shade, no shine, no butterflies, no bees,
No fruits, no flowers, no leaves, no birds,
November!

Thomas Hood

Cheltenham Waters

Here I lie with my three daughters,
Died of drinking Cheltenham Waters.
Had we stuck to Epsom Salts
We would not be in these 'ere vaults.

Anonymous

The Adventures of Little Katy

Little Katy wandered where
  She espied a Grizzly Bear.
Noticing his savage wrath,
  Katy kicked him from her path.

Little Katy, darling child,
  Met a Leopard, fierce and wild;
Ere the ugly creature sped off,
  Little Katy bit his head off.

Katy, in her best blue cape,
  Met a furious angry Ape;
But his rage received a check, –
  Little Katy wrung his neck.

Little Katy met a Lion;
  From starvation he was dyin'.
Though misfortune hadn't crushed him,
  Katy stepped on him and squashed him.

Little Katy, near the Niger,
  Met a big, blood-thirsty Tiger;
Tied a brick around his throat,
  Went and drowned him in the moat.

Little Katy had a fuss
  With a Hippopotamus;
Though the beast was somewhat weighty,
  He was soon knocked out by Katy.

Little Katy flushed with ire
  As a hungry Wolf came nigh her.
So impertinent was he,
  Katy chased him up a tree.

Little Katy, once by chance
  Met a drove of Elephants;
Katy, fearing they might crowd her,
  Scattered round some Persian powder.

Carolyn Wells

Duet for Mole and Worm

'Kindly do,' said the Mole,
'not obstruct the Public Hole.'
'Forgive me,' said the Worm, 'for being blind.'

'You will find,' said the Mole,
'(if you practise self control)
the lack will not debilitate your mind.'

'But my mind,' cried the Worm,
'(as my parents will confirm)
is squeeze'n'squirm anoptically combined.'

'Yet designed,' said the Mole,
'for a Great Symbolic Rôle.'
'Do you think so, Mole?' said Worm. 'How very kind.'

      Chorus:
'Freeze the lake! Frost the grass!
Through the Underworld we pass,
a-busy-be-low-burrow-iggl-kin!'
'You know,' said the Mole, 'where you are—in a hole:
if you do not meet each other coming out,
you are sure to meet each other going in.'

      (They strut)
M: 'How pitiful, dear Worm, to be a human . . .'
W: 'Creation's only wrinkle, Mole! Poor man . . .'
M: 'Imagine every day bar one day Monday . . .'
W: 'Part beef, part bluff, part pique, part marzipan . . .'

      Chorus:
'Me the First! PhD!
Failed to make it in a tree!
While-we-go-busy-borrow-iggle-kin!'
'You know,' said the Mole, 'where you are—in a hole:
if you do not meet each other coming out,
you are sure to meet each other going in.'

                        Christopher Logue

The Welsh

The gallant Welsh, of all degrees,
  Have one delightful habit:
They cover toast with melted cheese,
  And call the thing a rabbit.

And though no fur upon it grows,
And though it has no twitching nose,
  Nor twinkling tail behind it,
As reputable rabbits should;
Yet taste a piece, and very good,
  I'm bound to say, you'll find it.

                              E. V. Lucas

Susan Simpson

Sudden swallows, swiftly skimming,
    Sunset's slowly spreading shade,
Silvery songsters sweetly singing,
    Summer's soothing serenade.

Susan Simpson strolled sedately,
    Stifling sobs, suppressing sighs.
Seeing Stephen Slocum, stately
    She stopped, showing some surprise.

'Say,' said Stephen, 'sweetest sigher;
    Say, shall Stephen spouseless stay ?'
Susan, seeming somewhat shyer,
    Showed submissiveness straightway.

Summer's season slowly stretches,
    Susan Simpson Slocum she –
So she signed some simple sketches –
    Soul sought soul successfully.

Six Septembers Susan swelters;
    Six sharp seasons snow supplies;
Susan's satin sofa shelters
    Six small Slocums side by side.

Anonymous

Little Willie

Little Willie from his mirror
Licked the mercury right off,
Thinking, in his childish error,
It would cure the whooping cough.

At the funeral his mother
Brightly said to Mrs Brown:
''Twas a chilly day for Willie
When the mercury went down!'

Anonymous

28

Tring

There was an old lady from Tring
Who replied when they asked her to sing
    'You may find it odd
    But I cannot tell *God*
Save the Weasel from *Pop goes the King*'

Anonymous

Crying Jack

Once a little boy, Jack, was, oh! ever so good,
Till he took a strange notion to cry all he could.

So he cried all the day, and he cried all the night,
He cried in the morning and in the twilight;

He cried till his voice was as hoarse as a crow,
And his mouth grew so large it looked like a great O.

It grew at the bottom and grew at the top;
It grew till they thought that it never would stop.

Each day his great mouth grew taller and taller,
And his dear little self grew smaller and smaller.

At last, that same mouth grew so big that – alack! –
It was only a mouth with a border of Jack.

Anonymous

Twickenham

There was a young lady of Twickenham,
Whose boots were too tight to walk quickenham.
    She bore them awhile,
    But at last, at a stile,
She pulled them both off and was sickenham.

Anonymous

Thessaly

There was a Man of Thessaly,
And he was wondrous wise:
He jumped into a briar hedge
And scratched out both his eyes.
But when he saw his eyes were out,
With all his might and main
He jumped into another hedge
And scratched them in again.

Anonymous

The Sleepy Giant

My age is three hundred and seventy-two,
    And I think, with the deepest regret,
How I used to pick up and voraciously chew
    The dear little boys whom I met.

I've eaten them raw, in their holiday suits;
    I've eaten them curried with rice;
I've eaten them baked, in their jackets and boots,
    And found them exceedingly nice.

But now that my jaws are too weak for such fare,
    I think it exceedingly rude
To do such a thing, when I'm quite well aware
    Little boys do not like to be chewed.

And so I contentedly live upon eels,
    And try to do nothing amiss,
And I pass all the time I can spare from my meals
    In innocent slumber – like this.

Charles Edward Carryl

The Habits of the Hippopotamus

The hippopotamus is strong
   And huge of head and broad of bustle;
The limbs on which he rolls along
   Are big with hippopotomuscle.

He does not greatly care for sweets
   Like ice cream, apple pie, or custard,
But takes to flavor what he eats
   A little hippopotomustard.

The hippopotamus is true
   To all his principles, and just;
He always tries his best to do
   The things one hippopotomust.

He never rides in trucks or trams,
   In taxicabs or omnibuses,
And so keeps out of traffic jams
   And other hippopotomusses.

Arthur Guiterman

Maria Jane

It really gives me heartfelt pain
To tell you of Maria Jane,
For oh! she was so naughty!
Her nurse would weep and say: 'Ah me!
If you're so bad when only three,
What will you be at forty ?'

She loved to paddle in the wet
'Till soaked with mud her clothes would get,
For oh! she was so dirty!
Her nurse would weep and cry: 'Ah me!
If you love dirt so much at three,
What will you love at thirty ?'

Her appetite did all surprise,
Plum puddings, cakes and hot mince-pies,
For oh! she ne'er had plenty!
Her nurse would weep and scream: 'Ah me!
If you can eat so much at three,
What will you eat at twenty ?'

Alfred Scott-Gatty

The Sunday Fisherman

A fisherman, on angling bent,
One Sabbath morning left his tent.

    The Tent, ∧

He took his can, and very quick
He dug his fish-worms with a pick.

    The Pick, ⊢ The Worms, ∽∽

He thought he'd try for bass and smelt,
And fixed his fish-bag to his belt.

    The Belt, ◡ The Bag, ◠

In case some fish of size he'd get,
He took along his landing net.

The Landing Net, ⊓

As fishermen get very dry,
They always have a flask hard by.

The Flask, ⌀

As fishermen get hungry, too,
Of pretzels he procured a few.

The Pretzels, ଷଷଷଷ

Some lines he took along on spools
To teach them to the finny schools.

The Spools, ⊢ ⊢ ⊢

He had some entertaining books
Of highly-tempered Limerick hooks.

The Hooks, JJJ

And thus prepared, he got his boat,
And out upon the stream did float.

The Boat, ⊔

Whene'er the wind began to fail
He used the paddle with the sail.

The Paddle, ◁⊃

He stopped to fish, among the sedge,
A mile or so below the bridge.

The Bridge, ⊓⊓⊓⊓⊓◥

Some bites he straight began to get,
It was the gallinippers bit.

The Gallinippers, ⋎⋎⋎⋎

One of his lines spun off the reel;
He landed in the boat an eel.

The Eel, ∽

Then quickly it began to rain,
But his umbrella was in vain.

The Umbrella, ⊤

Above his head the thunder crashed,
And all around the lightning flashed.

The Lightning, ⩾

The storm blew, and the boat upset;
The man went down into the wet.

The Upturned Boat, ⌐⌐

And as he sank, his bubbles rose,
Smaller and smaller toward the close.

The Bubbles, O O O o o o

Oh, Sunday fishers, old and young,
You will get drowned, or you'll get hung!

The Gallows, ⊓

A. W. Bellaw

Woffsky-Poffsky

Woffsky-Poffsky, Woffsky-Poffsky,
Once he was a Cossack hetman:
But he fell into the Dnieper,
And became a Cossack wet-man.

Laura E. Richards

The Penguin Bold

To see the penguin out at sea,
   And watch how he behaves,
Would prove that penguins cannot be
   And never shall be slaves.
You haven't got a notion
How penguins brave the ocean,
   And laugh with scorn at waves.

To see the penguin at his ease
   Performing fearful larks
With stingarees of all degrees,
   As well as whales and sharks;
The sight would quickly let you know
The great contempt that penguins show
   For stingarees and sharks.

O see the penguin as he goes
   A-turning Catherine wheels,
Without repose upon the nose
   Of walruses and seals.
But bless your heart, a penguin feels
Supreme contempt for foolish seals,
   While he never fails, where'er he goes,
   To turn back-flips on a walrus nose.

Norman Lindsay

You!

I've come from a Land that lies over the Seas,
Where the Oysters grow upon Apple-trees;
And I've sailed for a year without Victuals or Rest,
Trying to find out a Blue-bottle's Nest.
I found only a couple of Flounders in fits,
And a grey-headed Cockle gone out of his wits;
But the ugliest Creature I've found, it is true,
I can spell in three letters – that's Y-O-U – you.

Charles Henry Ross

Eletelephony

Once there was an elephant,
Who tried to use the telephant –
No! no! I mean an elephone
Who tried to use the telephone –
(Dear me! I am not certain quite
That even now I've got it right.)

Howe'er it was, he got his trunk
Entangled in the telephunk;
The more he tried to get it free,
The louder buzzed the telephee –
(I fear I'd better drop the song
Of elephop and telephong!)

Laura E. Richards

Hannah Bantry

Hannah Bantry, in the pantry,
Gnawing a mutton bone;
    How she gnawed it!
    How she clawed it!
When she found herself alone.

Anonymous

I'm a Treble in the Choir

In the Choir I'm a treble
And my singing is the debbel!
I'm a treble in the Choir!
They sing high but I sing higher.
Treble singing's VERY high,
But the highest high am I!
Soon I'll burst like any bubble:
I'm a treble – that's the trouble!

Edmond Kapp

The Boy

The boy stood on the burning deck,
His feet were full of blisters;
The flames came up and burned his pants,
And now he wears his sister's.

Anonymous

Incidents in the Life of My Uncle Arly

O my agèd Uncle Arly!
Sitting on a heap of Barley
    Thro' the silent hours of night, –
Close beside a leafy thicket: –
On his nose there was a Cricket, –
In his hat a Railway-Ticket; –
    (But his shoes were far too tight.)

Long ago, in youth, he squander'd
All his goods away, and wander'd
    To the Tiniskoop-hills afar.
There on golden sunsets blazing,
Every evening found him gazing, –
Singing, – 'Orb! you're quite amazing!
    'How I wonder what you are!'

Like the ancient Medes and Persians,
Always by his own exertions
    He subsisted on those hills; –
Whiles, – by teaching children spelling, –
Or at times by merely yelling, –
Or at intervals by selling
    Propter's Nicodemus Pills.

Later, in his morning rambles
He perceived the moving brambles –
    Something square and white disclose; –
'Twas a First-class Railway-Ticket;
But, on stooping down to pick it
Off the ground, – a pea-green Cricket
    Settled on my uncle's Nose.

Never – never more, – oh! never,
Did that Cricket leave him ever, –
    Dawn or evening, day or night; –
Clinging as a constant treasure, –
Chirping with a cheerious measure, –
Wholly to my uncle's pleasure, –
    (Though his shoes were far too tight.)

So for three-and-forty winters,
Till his shoes were worn to splinters,
    All those hills he wander'd o'er, –
Sometimes silent; – sometimes yelling; –
Till he came to Borley-Melling,
Near his old ancestral dwelling; –
    (But his feet were far too sore.)

On a little heap of Barley
Died my agèd uncle Arly,
    And they buried him one night; –
Close beside the leafy thicket; –
There, – his hat and Railway-Ticket; –
There, – his ever-faithful Cricket; –
    (But his shoes were far too tight.)

Edward Lear

Doubt

I sometimes think I'd rather crow
And be a rooster than to roost
And be a crow. But I dunno.

A rooster he can roost also,
Which don't seem fair when crows can't crow.
Which may help, some. Still I dunno.

Crows should be glad of one thing, though;
Nobody thinks of eating crow,
While roosters they are good enough
For anyone unless they're tough.

There are lots of tough old roosters though,
And anyway a crow can't crow,
So mebby roosters stand more show.
It looks that way. But I dunno.

Anonymous

Sparta

A musical student from Sparta
Was a truly magnificent farter;
    On the strength of one bean
    He'd fart *God Save The Queen*,
And Beethoven's *Moonlight Sonata*.

Anonymous

Mr Prop

There was a man who built a house,
    And when the winds began to grumble,
He with his shoulder propped it up,
    For much he feared that it would tumble.
He propped it up throughout the day,
    Till it was time to go to bed,
But as he blew the candle out,
    The roof fell down upon his head.

Charles Henry Ross

Prudence Pedantic

Prudence Pedantic,
She nearly went frantic
Because her small nephew said, ''Taint!'
But when her big brother
Said 'Hain't got none, nuther!'
She fell on the floor in a faint.

Laura E. Richards

The Train to Glasgow

Here is the train to Glasgow.

Here is the driver,
Mr MacIver,
Who drove the train to Glasgow.

Here is the guard from Donibristle
Who waved his flag and blew his whistle
To tell the driver,
Mr MacIver,
To start the train to Glasgow.

Here is a boy called Donald MacBrain
Who came to the station to catch the train
But saw the guard from Donibristle
Wave his flag and blow his whistle
To tell the driver,
Mr MacIver,
To start the train to Glasgow.

Here is the guard, a kindly man
Who, at the last moment, hauled into the van
That fortunate boy called Donald MacBrain
Who came to the station to catch the train
But saw the guard from Donibristle
Wave his flag and blow his whistle
To tell the driver,
Mr MacIver,
To start the train to Glasgow.

Here are hens and here are cocks,
Clucking and crowing inside a box,
In charge of the guard, that kindly man
Who, at the last moment, hauled into the van
That fortunate boy called Donald MacBrain
Who came to the station to catch the train
But saw the guard from Donibristle
Wave his flag and blow his whistle
To tell the driver,
Mr MacIver,
To start the train to Glasgow.

Here is the train. It gave a jolt
Which loosened a catch and loosened a bolt,
And let out the hens and let out the cocks,
Clucking and crowing out of their box,
In charge of the guard, that kindly man
Who, at the last moment, hauled into the van
That fortunate boy called Donald MacBrain

Who came to the station to catch the train
But saw the guard from Donibristle
Wave his flag and blow his whistle.
To tell the driver,
Mr MacIver,
To start the train to Glasgow.

The guard chased a hen and, missing it, fell.
The hens were all squawking, the cocks were as well,
And unless you were there you haven't a notion
The flurry, the fuss, the noise and commotion
Caused by the train which gave a jolt
And loosened a catch and loosened a bolt
And let out the hens and let out the cocks,
Clucking and crowing out of their box,
In charge of the guard, that kindly man
Who, at the last moment, hauled into the van
That fortunate boy called Donald MacBrain
Who came to the station to catch the train
But saw the guard from Donibristle
Wave his flag and blow his whistle
To tell the driver,
Mr MacIver,
To start the train to Glasgow.

Now Donald was quick and Donald was neat
And Donald was nimble on his feet.
He caught the hens and he caught the cocks
And he put them back in their great big box.
The guard was pleased as pleased could be
And invited Donald to come to tea
On Saturday, at Donibristle,
And let him blow his lovely whistle,
And said in all his life he'd never
Seen a boy so quick and clever,
And so did the driver,
Mr MacIver,
Who drove the train to Glasgow.

Wilma Horsbrugh

Old Joe Clarke

Old Joe Clarke, he had a house,
Was fifteen stories high,
And every darn room in that house
Was full of chicken pie.

I went down to Old Joe Clarke's
And found him eating supper;
I stubbed my toe on the table leg
And stuck my nose in the butter.

I went down to Old Joe Clarke's
But Old Joe wasn't in;
I sat right down on the red-hot stove
And got right up again.

Old Joe Clarke had a candy box
To keep his sweetheart in;
He'd take her out and kiss her twice
And put her back again.

Anonymous

The Emu

The Emu makes, though prone to fret,
A quite accommodating pet.
By dint of arduous explaining –
And tactful and intensive training
It may be taught a mild routine
To lighten the domestic scene –
To peg the clothes – to draw a phaeton –
To greet such guests it has to wait on –
To tile the roof – to polish floors
And other preferential chores.
In doing jobs like these, the Emu
Will grow to cherish and esteem you.

Leon Gellert

The Polar Bear's Party
or
The Mannerless Musk Ox

A hospitable Polar Bear
   Resolved to give a party;
His nature was gregarious,
   His sentiments were hearty.

He asked the Walruses and Seals
   That lived upon the floe;
And in a burst of friendliness
   The Musky Ox also.

'The Musky Ox he lives on land,
   But still, he likes it cold;
His fur is thick, he's never sick;
   I think I'll make so bold!'

'O Musky Ox, O Husky Ox,
   Your neighbor, Polar Bear,
Invites you to his party;
   He hopes you'll come; so there!'

A lovely feast of blubber strips
   He set before each guest,
A puffin pie, a stuffin' pie,
   And boobies of the best.

They drank – I don't know what they drank,
   But they were blithe and gay,
And still the more the viands shrank,
   The more they had to say.

All, all except the Musky Ox!
   He sat beside the board;
He did not eat, he did not drink,
   He did not speak a word.

'Speak up! speak up! thou Musky Ox,
    Why sit so dumb and still?
The rest are merry as you please,
    And eat and drink their fill.'

The Musk Ox raised his musky eyes,
    And shook his musky head;
'I don't like blubber, you ursine lubber,'
    He very rudely said.

'Your puffin pie, your stuffin' pie,
    They fill me with disgust,
Bring me, old hoss, some Iceland moss!
    You will, you shall, you must!'

The Bear looked at the Walruses,
    And they looked back at him,
They rose beside the festal board,
    And oh, their looks were grim.

'Go seek your Iceland moss yourself,
    You rude unmannered beast;
It will be long before you're asked
    To share a Polar feast!'

They seized upon that Musky Ox,
    And drove him to the shore;
They bundled him, they trundled him,
    With loud and angry roar.

Now see him wallop o'er the snow,
    Hungry and tired and cross,
For not within a hundred miles
    Grew any Iceland moss.

While Bear and Walruses and Seals
    Cry, 'Wherefore all this fuss?
E'en let him go, old Double-Toe!
    There's all the more for us!'

Laura E. Richards

Miss Banker

There was a young lady called Banker,
Who slept while the ship lay at anchor,
  But woke in dismay
  When she heard the mate say,
'Now hoist up the top-sheet and spanker.'

Anonymous

Little Miss Boddle

Little Miss Boddle
Is so Fat she can't toddle.
If she had any Sense in her Noddle,
She'd waddle.

Charles Henry Ross

How to Treat Grandma

When grandma visits you, my dears,
    Be good as you can be;
Don't put hot waffles in her ears,
    Or beetles in her tea.

Don't sew a pattern on her cheek
    With worsted or with silk;
Don't call her naughty names in Greek,
    Or spray her face with milk.

Don't drive a staple in her foot,
    Don't stick pins in her head;
And, oh, I beg you, do not put
    Live embers in her bed.

These things are not considered kind;
    They worry her, and tease –
Such cruelty is not refined
    It always fails to please.

Be good to grandma, little chaps,
    Whatever else you do;
And then she'll grow to be – perhaps –
    More tolerant of you.

Anonymous

Bishopsgate

Bishopsgate Without!
Bishopsgate Within!
What a clamour at the Gate,
O what a din!
Inside and Outside
The Bishops bang and shout,
Outside crying, 'Let me In!'
Inside, 'Let me Out!'

Eleanor Farjeon

Two Epitaphs

Mrs Shoven

Underneath this crust
Lies the mouldering dust
Of ELEANOR BATCHELOR SHOVEN,
   Well versed in the Arts
   Of pies, custards, and tarts,
And the lucrative trade of the oven.
   When she'd lived long enough
   She made her last puff,
A puff by her husband much praised,
   And now she doth lie
   And make a dirt pie,
In hopes that her crust may be raised.

Anonymous

Bones

Said Mr Smith, 'I really cannot
   Tell you, Dr Jones –
The most peculiar pain I'm in –
   I think it's in my *bones*.'

Said Dr Jones, 'Oh, Mr Smith,
   That's nothing. Without doubt
We have a simple cure for that;
   It is to take them out.'

He laid forthwith poor Mr Smith
   Close-clamped upon the table,
And, cold as stone, took out his bone
   As fast as he was able.

And Smith said, 'Thank you, thank you, thank you,'
   And wished him a Good-day;
And with his parcel 'neath his arm
   He slowly moved away.

Walter de la Mare

The Old Nag's Song

It's very confining, this living in stables,
   And passing one's time among wagons and carts;
I much prefer dining at gentlemen's tables,
   And living on turkeys and cranberry tarts.

I find with surprise that I'm constantly sneezing;
   I'm stiff in the legs, and I'm often for sale;
And the blue-bottle flies, with their tiresome teasing,
   Are quite out of reach of my weary old tail.

As spry as a kid and as trim as a spider
   Was I in the days of the Turnip-top Hunt,
When I used to get rid of the weight of my rider
   And canter contentedly in at the front.

I never was told that this jocular feature
   Of mine was a trick reprehensibly rude,
And yet I was sold, like a commonplace creature,
   To work in a circus for lodgings and food.

Pray why, if you please, should a capable charger
   Perform on a ladder and prance in a show?
And why should his knees be made thicker and larger
   By teaching him tricks that he'd rather not know?

Oh! why should a horse, for society fitted,
   Be doomed to employment so utterly bad,
And why should a coarse-looking man be permitted
   To dance on his back on a top-heavy pad?

It made me a wreck, with no hope of improvement,
   Too feeble to race with an invalid crab;
I'm wry in the neck, with a rickety movement
   Peculiarly suited for drawing a cab.

They pinch me with straps, and they bruise me with buckles,
   They drive me too rapidly over the stones; –
A reason, perhaps, why a number of knuckles
   Have lately appeared on my prominent bones.

I dream of a spot which I used to roam over
  In infancy's days, with a frolicsome skip,
Content with my lot, which was planted with clover,
  And never annoyed by the crack of a whip.

But I think my remarks will determine the question,
  Of why I am bony and thin as a rail;
I'm off for some larks, to improve my digestion,
  And point the stern moral conveyed by my tail.

Charles Edward Carryl

Hats

I put my hat upon my head
  And walked along the Strand,
And there I met another man
  Whose hat was in his hand.

Samuel Johnson

The Hippopotamus

I shoot the Hippopotamus
With bullets made of platinum,
Because if I use leaden ones
His hide is sure to flatten 'em.

Hilaire Belloc

Bores

The greatest Bore is Boredom
  But the greatest Boredom known
Is the Bore who talks about himself★
  And *his* affairs alone
When you want *him* to listen
  While you talk about your own.

Anonymous

★ *Or herself.*

The Old False Leg

Three crows hopped on an old false leg,
   On an old false leg,
   An old false leg,
Three crows hopped on an old false leg
   Which lay out alone on the moor.

Whoever could have dropped that old false leg,
   Old false leg,
   That old false leg,
Whoever could have dropped that old false leg
   Out by the lake on the moor?

It was nobody dropped that old false leg,
   Old false leg,
   Old false leg,
It was nobody dropped that very false leg,
   Which slept out alone on the moor.

That old false leg jumped up on its toes,
   Up on its toes,
   Up on its toes,
That old false leg jumped up on its toes,
   In the very wet mist on the moor,

And it hit the tail feathers off those crows,
   Off those crows,
   Off those crows,
And it hit the tail feathers off those crows,
   Caw, caw, caw on the moor.

And those crows flew away quite nakedly,
   Quite nakedly,
   Quite nakedly,
And those crows flew away quite nakedly,
   Into the mist on the moor.

And the false leg thereupon strolled to the shore,
   Strolled to the shore,
   Strolled to the shore,
And the false leg thereupon strolled to the shore,
   Into the lake, and was seen no more.

        Geoffrey Grigson

Hengist and Horsa

Hengist was coarser than Horsa,
And Horsa was awfully coarse.
Horsa drank whiskey,
Told tales that were risqué,
But Hengist was in a divorce.
Horsa grew coarser and coarser,
But Hengist was coarse all his life.
That reprobate Horsa
Drank tea from a saucer,
But Hengist ate peas with his knife.

Desmond Carter

Mr Vague

Once – but no matter when –
      There lived – no matter where –
A man, whose name – but then
      I need not that declare.

He – well, he had been born,
      And so he was alive;
His age – I details scorn –
      Was somethingty and five.

He lived – how many years
      I truly can't decide;
But this one fact appears
      He lived – until he died.

'He died,' I have averred,
      But cannot prove 'twas so,
But that he was interred,
      At any rate, I know.

I fancy he'd a son,
      I hear he had a wife:
Perhaps he'd more than one,
      I know not, on my life!

But whether he was rich,
      Or whether he was poor,
Or neither – both – or which,
      I cannot say, I'm sure.

I can't recall his name,
      Or what he used to do:
But then – well, such is fame!
      'Twill so serve me and you.

And that is why I thus,
      About this unknown man
Would fain create a fuss,
      To rescue, if I can

From dark oblivion's blow,
　　Some record of his lot:
But, ah! I do not know
　　Who – where – when – why – or what.

MORAL

In this brief pedigree
　　A moral we should find –
But what it ought to be
　　Has quite escaped my mind!

Anonymous

On a Poor Woman

Here lies a poor woman who always was tired,
　　She lived in a house where no help wasn't hired.
The last words she said were 'Dear friends, I am going,
　　Where washing ain't wanted, nor mending, nor sewing.
There all things is done just exact to my wishes,
　　For where folk don't eat there's no washing of dishes.
In Heaven loud anthems for ever are ringing,
　　But having no voice, I'll keep clear of the singing.
Don't mourn for me now, don't mourn for me never;
　　I'm going to do nothing for ever and ever.'

Anonymous

Mr Ody

Mr Ody met a body
Hanging from a tree;
And what was worse
He met a hearse
As black as black could be.
Mr Ody said: 'By God, he
Ought to have a ride!'
Said the driver: 'I'd oblige yer,
But we're full inside!'

E. Nesbit

The Walrus and the Carpenter

The sun was shining on the sea,
    Shining with all his might:
He did his very best to make
    The billows smooth and bright –
And this was odd, because it was
    The middle of the night.

The moon was shining sulkily,
    Because she thought the sun
Had got no business to be there
    After the day was done –
'It's very rude of him,' she said,
    'To come and spoil the fun!'

The sea was wet as wet could be,
    The sands were dry as dry.
You could not see a cloud, because
    No cloud was in the sky:
No birds were flying overhead –
    There were no birds to fly.

The Walrus and the Carpenter
    Were walking close at hand;
They wept like anything to see
    Such quantities of sand:
'If this were only cleared away,'
    They said, 'it *would* be grand!'

'If seven maids with seven mops
    Swept it for half a year,
Do you suppose,' the Walrus said,
    'That they could get it clear?'
'I doubt it,' said the Carpenter,
    And shed a bitter tear.

'O Oysters, come and walk with us!'
    The Walrus did beseech.
'A pleasant walk, a pleasant talk,
    Along the briny beach:
We cannot do with more than four,
    To give a hand to each.'

The eldest Oyster looked at him,
    But never a word he said:
The eldest Oyster winked his eye,
    And shook his heavy head –
Meaning to say he did not choose
    To leave the oyster-bed.

But four young Oysters hurried up,
    All eager for the treat:
Their coats were brushed, their faces washed,
    Their shoes were clean and neat –
And this was odd, because, you know,
    They hadn't any feet.

Four other Oysters followed them,
    And yet another four;
And thick and fast they came at last,
    And more, and more, and more –
All hopping through the frothy waves,
    And scrambling to the shore.

The Walrus and the Carpenter
    Walked on a mile or so,
And then they rested on a rock
    Conveniently low:
And all the little Oysters stood
    And waited in a row.

'The time has come,' the Walrus said,
    'To talk of many things:
Of shoes – and ships – and sealing-wax –
    Of cabbages – and kings –
And why the sea is boiling hot –
    And whether pigs have wings.'

'But wait a bit,' the Oysters cried,
    'Before we have our chat;
For some of us are out of breath,
    And all of us are fat!'
'No hurry!' said the Carpenter.
    They thanked him much for that.

'A loaf of bread,' the Walrus said,
    'Is what we chiefly need:
Pepper and vinegar besides
    Are very good indeed –
Now if you're ready, Oysters dear,
    We can begin to feed.'

'But not on us!' the Oysters cried,
    Turning a little blue.
'After such kindness, that would be
    A dismal thing to do!'
'The night is fine,' the Walrus said,
    'Do you admire the view?

'It was so kind of you to come!
    And you are very nice!'
The Carpenter said nothing but
    'Cut us another slice:
I wish you were not quite so deaf –
    I've had to ask you twice!'

'It seems a shame,' the Walrus said,
    'To play them such a trick,
After we've brought them out so far,
    And made them trot so quick!'
The Carpenter said nothing but
    'The butter's spread too thick!'

'I weep for you,' the Walrus said:
    'I deeply sympathize.'
With sobs and tears he sorted out
    Those of the largest size,
Holding his pocket-handkerchief
    Before his streaming eyes.

'O Oysters,' said the Carpenter,
    'You've had a pleasant run!
Shall we be trotting home again?'
    But answer came there none –
And this was scarcely odd, because
    They'd eaten every one.

                                    Lewis Carroll

To Lizzie, My Old Car

I love you though your radiator's busted,
   I love you though your gudgeon pins are worn;
I love you though your piston-rings all rattle,
   I love you though your hood is frayed and torn;
I love you though your carburetter hisses,
   I love you though your wheels won't run in line;
I love you though your oil tank's always leaking –
   I love you, yes, I love you, Lizzie mine.

I love you though your steering gear is faulty,
   I love you though your body creaks and groans;
I love you though your hooter's ceased from hooting,
   I love you though your differential moans;
I love you though your big-ends all are knocking,
   I love you though your tail-light fails to shine;
I love you though your cushion's hard as blazes –
   I love you, yes, I love you, Lizzie mine.

I love you though your king bolts need rebushing,
   I love you though your wind-screen lets in rain;
I love you though your clutch is always slipping,
   I love you though to start you gives me pain;
I love you though your generator's crippled,
   I love you though your intake pipe does whine;
I love you though your spark plugs all are missing –
   I love you, yes, I love you, Lizzie mine.

I love you though your brushes do not function,
   I love you though your valve springs all are poor;
I love you though you're fused in both your headlights,
   I love you though I cannot shut your door;
I love you though your paint has lost its lustre,
   I love you though your nickel's lost its shine;
With all your faults, you fickle jade, I love you –
   I love you, yes, I love you, Lizzie mine.

Anonymous

The ABC

'Twas midnight in the schoolroom
And every desk was shut,
When suddenly from the alphabet
Was heard a loud 'Tut-tut!'

Said A to B, 'I don't like C;
His manners are a lack.
For all I ever see of C
Is a semi-circular back!'

'I disagree,' said D to B,
'I've never found C so.
From where I stand, he seems to be
An uncompleted O.'

C was vexed, 'I'm much perplexed,
You criticize my shape.
I'm made like that, to help spell Cat
And Cow and Cool and Cape.'

'He's right,' said E; said F, 'Whoopee!'
Said G, ''Ip, 'ip, 'ooray!'
'You're dropping me,' roared H to G,
'Don't do it please I pray!'

'Out of my way,' L said to K.
'I'll make poor I look ILL.'
To stop this stunt, J stood in front,
And presto! ILL was JILL.

'U know,' said V, 'that W
Is twice the age of me,
For as a Roman V is five
I'm half as young as he.'

X and Y yawned sleepily,
'Look at the time!' they said.
'Let's all get off to beddy byes.'
They did, then 'Z-z-z.'

X and Y yawned sleepily,
'Look at the time!' they said.
They all jumped in to beddy byes
And the last one in was Z.

Spike Milligan

Of The Convicts sent to Australia

True patriots we – for be it understood
We left our country for our country's good.

Barrington the Pickpocket

The Giraffe

You must not chaff
The tall Giraffe
About his size of collars,
Nor watch him drink,
And rudely wink
And ask him how he swallers.

When at the Zoo
It will not do
To criticise his spots,
Nor ask him when
You pass his pen
To tie his neck in knots.

Nor is it nice
To give advice
On troubles of the spine –
The tall Giraffe
Enjoys a laugh,
But there he draws the line.

John Joy Bell

Nathan Nobb

Nathan Nobb,
Oh, what a job!
Always walked on his head;
His mother would sob
To his brother Bob,
And his father took to his bed.

They made him a boot
His head to suit,
But a horrible thing must be said, –
His hair took root,
And began to shoot,
One day, in the garden bed!

So there he stands
With the help of his hands
And a little support from his nose:
The gardener man,
With the watering-can,
Says, 'Gracious, how fast he grows!'

W. B. Rands

FISONS No 1
BIGHEAD

Mr Finney's Turnip

Mr Finney had a turnip
   And it grew and it grew;
And it grew behind the barn,
   And that turnip did no harm.

There it grew and it grew
   Till it could grow no longer;
Then his daughter Lizzie picked it
   And put it in the cellar.

There it lay and it lay
   Till it began to rot;
And his daughter Susie took it
   And put it in the pot.

And they boiled it and boiled it
   As long as they were able,
And then his daughters took it
   And put it on the table.

Mr Finney and his wife
   They sat down to sup;
And they ate and they ate
   And they ate that turnip up.

Anonymous

Margery Maggot

Margery Maggot,
She lighted a faggot,
To cook a repast for her cat.
But instead of a bone,
She made soup of a stone,
And gave the poor animal that.

Laura E. Richards

My Sister Clarissa spits twice if I kiss her

My sister Clarissa spits twice if I kiss her
and once if I hold her hand.
I reprimand her – my name's Alexander –
for spitting I simply can't stand.

'Clarissa, Clarissa, my sister, is this a
really nice habit to practise?'
But she always replies with innocent eyes
rather softly, 'Dear Brother, the fact is

I think I'm an ape with a very small grape
crushed to juice in my mastodon lips.
Since I am not a prude, though I hate being rude,
I am simply ejecting the pips.'

George Barker

Macavity: The Mystery Cat

Macavity's a Mystery Cat: he's called the Hidden Paw –
For he's the master criminal who can defy the Law.
He's the bafflement of Scotland Yard, the Flying Squad's despair:
For when they reach the scene of crime – *Macavity's not there!*

Macavity, Macavity, there's no one like Macavity,
He's broken every human law, he breaks the law of gravity.
His powers of levitation would make a fakir stare,
And when you reach the scene of crime – *Macavity's not there!*
You may seek him in the basement, you may look up in the air –
But I tell you once and once again, *Macavity's not there!*

Macavity's a ginger cat, he's very tall and thin;
You would know him if you saw him, for his eyes are sunken in.
His brow is deeply lined with thought, his head is highly domed;
His coat is dusty from neglect, his whiskers are uncombed.
He sways his head from side to side, with movements like a snake;
And when you think he's half asleep, he's always wide awake.

Macavity, Macavity, there's no one like Macavity,
For he's a fiend in feline shape, a monster of depravity.
You may meet him in a by-street, you may see him in the square –
But when a crime's discovered, then *Macavity's not there!*

He's outwardly respectable. (They say he cheats at cards.)
And his footprints are not found in any file of Scotland Yard's.
And when the larder's looted, or the jewel-case is rifled,
Or when the milk is missing, or another Peke's been stifled,
Or the greenhouse glass is broken, and the trellis past repair –
Ay, there's the wonder of the thing! *Macavity's not there!*

And when the Foreign Office find a Treaty's gone astray,
Or the Admiralty lose some plans and drawings by the way,
There may be a scrap of paper in the hall or on the stair –
But it's useless to investigate – *Macavity's not there!*
And when the loss has been disclosed, the Secret Service say:
'It *must* have been Macavity!' – but he's a mile away.
You'll be sure to find him resting, or a-licking of his thumbs,
Or engaged in doing complicated long division sums.

Macavity, Macavity, there's no one like Macavity,
There never was a Cat of such deceitfulness and suavity.
He always has an alibi, and one or two to spare:
At whatever time the deed took place – MACAVITY WASN'T THERE!
And they say that all the Cats whose wicked deeds are widely known
(I might mention Mungojerrie, I might mention Griddlebone)
Are nothing more than agents for the Cat who all the time
Just controls their operations: the Napoleon of Crime!

Thomas Stearns Eliot

Bengal

There once was a man of Bengal
Who was asked to a fancy dress ball;
    He murmured: 'I'll risk it
    and go as a biscuit . . . .'
But a dog ate him up in the hall.

Anonymous

The Lesser Lynx

The laughter of the Lesser Lynx
   Is often insincere:
It pays to be polite, he thinks,
   If Royalty is near.

So when the Lion steals his food
   Or kicks him from behind,
He smiles, of course – but oh, the rude
   Remarks that cross his mind!

E. V. Rieu

The Pelican

What a wonderful beast is the Pelican!
Whose bill can hold more than his belly can.
   He can take in his beak
   Enough food for a week –
I'm damned if I know how the hell he can.

Anonymous

Jack

That's Jack;
Lay a stick on his back!
What's he done? I cannot say.
We'll find out tomorrow,
And beat him today.

Charles Henry Ross

The Old Woman

There was an Old Woman who married a King,
But she had no Finger to put on the Ring,
So they bored a hole through her Nose instead,
And they say that it gave her a Cold in the Head.

Charles Henry Ross

Snores

'There's the cheeky snore, an' the squeaky snore, and the snore that
  sounds like silk;
There's the creamy, dreamy kind of snore that comes of drinkin'
  milk;
There's the raspy snore, an' the gaspy snore, an' the snore that's 'ard
  to wake,
An' the snore that's 'arf a jackass larf an' the hiss of a startled snake.
There's the snore that shows its owner's shick, an' the one that
  shows 'e's not,
And one 'oose owner I'd like to kick, the worst of all the lot.
It's a kind of cross between a calf an' a pig that's dyin' 'ard
With a bit thrown in from the mornin' din out in the poultry yard.

'There's also the snore that softly sighs like the close of an evenin'
  hymn,
As if a bloke 'ad just got wise 'e'd lorst an 'arf a jim.
I've 'eard 'em snore in concert pitch an' also a trifle flat,
With snores that orfen drop a stitch, then bustle an' get the bat.
There's the snore that trickles the keyhole track like onions bein'
  fried,
And the snore of the bachelor on 'ees back an' the spinster on 'er
  side.
There's the haughty snore an' the snorty snore of blokes wot's prim
  an proud,
An' the snore of the cove wot owes a score, 'oose conscience 'as 'im
  cowed!

E. G. Murphy

The Mad Grandpapa

Listen, little girls and boys;
    Listen, one and all!
Put away those nasty toys –
Mary, hold that horrid noise –
    Willy, drop your ball!
Come and listen, if you can,
To a bald but good old man.

Charley, if I call you twice,
    I shall box your ears!
Grandpapa has something nice
In the shape of good advice
    For his little dears:
Simple maxims for the young.
Mary, *will* you hold your tongue?

Folks will teach you when at school –
    'Never tell a lie!'
Nonsense: if you're not a fool
You may always break the rule,
    But you must be sly;
For they'll whip you, past a doubt,
If they ever find you out.

'Little boys,' they say, 'should be
    Seen but never heard!'
Rubbish: what can people see
In an ugly brat if he
    Never says a word?
Talk, then, if you feel inclin'd;
Talking shows the active mind.

Folks will tell you, 'Children *must*
    Do as they are bid;'
But you understand, I trust,
That the rule is quite unjust
    To a thoughtful kid:
For, if once brute force appears,
How about Free-will, my dears?

Folks say, 'Children should not let
    Angry passions rise.'
Humbug! When you're in a pet
Why on earth should you regret
    Blacking some one's eyes?
Children's eyes are made, in fact,
Just on purpose to be black'd.

I, when young, was green enough
    Blindly to obey
All the idiotic stuff
That an old pedantic muff
    Taught me day by day; –
And, you see – at eighty-five
I'm the biggest fool alive!

Henry Sambroke Leigh

The Monkeys

'This is a most degraded brute,'
    A lady once began,
'I never met a creature yet
    That was so like a man.'

And I replied: 'I must agree:
    Indeed, he's really human.
His wife's behind: I'm sure you'll find
    Her quite a pleasant woman.'

        [*Exit Lady*]

John Joy Bell

One Fine Day

One fine day in the middle of the night
Two dead men got up to fight;
Two blind men to see fair play,
Two dumb men to shout: 'Hurray!'
And two lame men to carry them away.

Anonymous

Hall and Knight
or
$$z + b + x = y + b + z$$

When he was young his cousins used to say of Mr Knight:
'This boy will write an Algebra – or looks as if he might.'
And sure enough, when Mr Knight had grown to be a man,
He purchased pen and paper and an inkpot, and began.

But he very soon discovered that he couldn't write at all,
And his heart was filled with yearnings for a certain Mr Hall;
Till, after many years of doubt, he sent his friend a card:
'Have tried to write an Algebra, but find it very hard.'

Now Mr Hall himself had tried to write a book for schools,
But suffered from a handicap: he didn't know the rules.
So when he heard from Mr Knight and understood his gist,
He answered him by telegram: 'Delighted to assist.'

So Mr Hall and Mr Knight they took a house together,
And they worked away at algebra in any kind of weather,
Determined not to give it up until they had evolved
A problem so constructed that it never could be solved.

'How hard it is,' said Mr Knight, 'to hide the fact from youth
That x and y are equal: it is such an obvious truth!'
'It is,' said Mr Hall, 'but if we gave a b to each,
We'd put the problem well beyond our little victims' reach.

Or are you anxious, Mr Knight, lest any boy should see
The utter superfluity of this repeated b?'
'I scarcely fear it,' he replied, and scratched his grizzled head,
'But perhaps it *would* be safer if to b we added z.'

'A brilliant stroke!' said Hall, and added z to either side;
Then looked at his accomplice with a flush of happy pride.
And Knight, he winked at Hall (a very pardonable lapse).
And they printed off the Algebra and sold it to the chaps.

E. V. Rieu

After a Visit to The Natural History Museum

This is the Wiggledywasticus,
   Very remarkable beast.
Nose to tail an eighth of a mile;
Took him an acre or two to smile;
Took him a quarter 'f an hour to wink;
Swallowed a pond for his morning drink.
Oh! would it had been vouchsafed to us
Upon the Wiggledywasticus
   Our wondering eyes to feast!

This is the Ptoodlecumtumpsydyl,
   Rather unusual bird.
Had a mouth before and behind;
Ate whichever way he'd a mind;
Spoiled his digestion, so they say,
Pindled and dwindled quite away,
Or else he might have been living still,
The singular Ptoodlecumtumpsydyl.
   A pity, upon my word!

This is the Ichthyosnortoryx,
   Truly astonishing fish.
Used to snort in a terrible way;
Scared the lobsters to death, they say;
Had a nose like a tea-kettle spout;
Broke it snorting, and so died out.
Sad! if he had n't got into this fix,
We might have made of the 'Snortoryx
   A very acceptable dish.

                    Laura E. Richards

The Akond of Swat

Who, or why, or which, or *what*, Is the Akond of SWAT ?
Is he tall or short, or dark or fair ?
Does he sit on a stool or a sofa or chair,
                              or SQUAT,
                    The Akond of Swat ?
Is he wise or foolish, young or old ?
Does he drink his soup and his coffee cold,
                              or HOT,
                    The Akond of Swat ?
Does he sing or whistle, jabber or talk,
And when riding abroad does he gallop or walk,
                              or TROT,
                    The Akond of Swat ?
Does he wear a turban, a fez, or a hat ?
Does he sleep on a mattress, a bed, or a mat,
                              or a COT,
                    The Akond of Swat ?
When he writes a copy in round-hand size,
Does he cross his T's and finish his I's
                        with a DOT,
                    The Akond of Swat ?
Can he write a letter concisely clear
Without a speck or a smudge or smear
                              or BLOT,
                    The Akond of Swat ?
Do his people like him extremely well ?
Or do they, whenever they can, rebel,
                              or PLOT,
                    At the Akond of Swat ?
If he catches them then, either old or young,
Does he have them chopped in pieces or hung,
                              or SHOT,
                    The Akond of Swat ?
Do his people prig in the lanes or park ?
Or even at times, when days are dark,
                              GAROTTE ?
                    O the Akond of Swat!
Does he study the wants of his own dominion ?
Or doesn't he care for public opinion
                              a JOT,
                    The Akond of Swat ?

To amuse his mind do his people show him
Pictures, or any one's last new poem,
                                 or WHAT,
                    For the Akond of Swat ?
At night if he suddenly screams and wakes,
Do they bring him only a few small cakes,
                                 or a LOT,
                    For the Akond of Swat ?
Does he live on turnips, tea, or tripe ?
Does he like his shawl to be marked with a stripe,
                                 or a DOT,
                    The Akond of Swat ?
Does he like to lie on his back in a boat
Like the lady who lived in that isle remote,
                                 SHALLOTT,
                    The Akond of Swat ?
Is he quiet, or always making a fuss ?
Is his steward a Swiss or a Swede or a Russ,
                                 or a SCOT,
                    The Akond of Swat ?
Does he like to sit by the calm blue wave ?
Or to sleep and snore in a dark green cave,
                                 or a GROTT,
                    The Akond of Swat ?
Does he drink small beer from a silver jug ?
Or a bowl ? or a glass ? or a cup ? or a mug ?
                                 or a POT.
                    The Akond of Swat ?
Does he beat his wife with a gold-topped pipe,
When she lets the gooseberries grow too ripe,
                                 or ROT,
                    The Akond of Swat ?
Does he wear a white tie when he dines with friends,
And tie it neat in a bow with ends,
                                 or a KNOT,
                    The Akond of Swat ?
Does he like new cream, and hate mince-pies ?
When he looks at the sun does he wink his eyes,
                                 or NOT,
                    The Akond of Swat ?
Does he teach his subjects to roast and bake ?

Does he sail about on an inland lake,
                    in a YACHT,
            The Akond of Swat?
Some one, or nobody, knows I wot
Who or which or why or what
                Is the Akond of Swat!

Edward Lear

A Reply from the Akond of Swat

Mr Lear, I'm the Akond of Swat;
    I am gracious and fat
    In a very tall hat
And I'm heating a very large pot –
You know why, and for whom, and for what.

Ethel Talbot Scheffauer

Samuel Pease

Under this sod and beneath these trees
Lies all that's left of Samuel Pease.
Pease ain't here,
It's just his pod;
He shelled out his soul
Which flew to God.

Anonymous

The Centipede

The Centipede was happy quite,
Until the Toad in fun
Said 'Pray which leg goes after which?'
And worked her mind to such a pitch,
She lay distracted in the ditch
Considering how to run.

Mrs Edmund Craster

Aunt Maud

I had written to Aunt Maud
Who was on a trip abroad,
When I heard she'd died of cramp
Just too late to save the stamp.

Anonymous

The Ballad of the Parrot and The Wig

The cat sat asleep by the fire,
    The mistress snored loud as a pig,
Jack took up his fiddle by Jenny's desire,
    And struck up a bit of a jig.

'Ods, bobs,' said the dame, jumping up from her chair,
    'Such music, dear Johnny, as that
Compels one to dance'; but John called out, 'Beware,
    Or you'll tread on the tail of the cat.'

The fiddler's kind warning proved totally vain,
    The happy old lady danced round,
She trod on poor pussy, who squall'd with the pain,
    And tumbled the dame to the ground.

'Why, Goody,' cried Gaffer, 'you're rather too big,
    Like a baby, to lie sprawling there.'
But while he thus joked her, Poll twitch'd off his wig,
    And left his poor noddle quite bare.

Poll flew with the prize quite delighted about,
    While Gaffer most loudly did roar;
When quick from the saucepan the pudding jump'd out,
    And danced in the sand on the floor.

The dame began laughing, the parrot laugh'd too;
    The pudding bounced open the door;
The door being open, Poll out of it flew,
    And they fear'd they should see her no more.

Poll flew with her prize to the top of a tree;
  Gaffer peppered its branches with stones;
And Goody, enraged that the parrot was free,
  Protested she'd break all her bones.

Gaffer went in a rage, and he did not keep cool,
  He said he would go for his gun;
And a host of young urchins, returning from school,
  Hurrah'd at the glorious fun.

Poll wickedly into a pond dropp'd the wig,
  By the side of which grew a tall tree;
Gaffer cut a long bough, and fish'd for his wig;
  And the boys danced and shouted with glee.

At last Gaffer managed to hook out his wig,
  Which suspended his desperate rage;
Jack struck up a tune, and they all danced a jig,
  And the parrot flew back to her cage.

Anonymous

Doctor Lettsom

If anybody comes to I,
  I physicks, bleeds, and sweats 'em;
If, after that, they like to die,
  Why, what care I ? –
  I Letts'm.

Anonymous

As I Was Coming Down the Stair

As I was coming down the stair
I met a man who wasn't there.
He wasn't there again to-day:
I *wish* that man would go away!

Anonymous

The Clam

You may leave the clam on the ocean floor,
    It's all the same to the clam,
For a hundred thousand years or more,
    It's all the same to the clam;
You may carry him home in a gunny sack,
And pour Tabasco on his back,
And use him for a midnight snack,
    It's all the same to the clam.

You may carry him 'round to bring you luck,
    It's all the same to the clam,
Or use him for a hockey puck,
    It's all the same to the clam.
You may dress him in the latest style,
Or pry him open with a file,
The clam will neither frown nor smile,
    It's all the same to the clam.

You may call him Bob, or Fran, or Nell,
    It's all the same to the clam;
Or make an ashtray from his shell,
    It's all the same to the clam;
You may take him riding on the train,
Or leave him sitting in the rain,
You'll never hear the clam complain,
    It's all the same to the clam.

So the world may stop, or the world may spin,
    It's all the same to the clam;
Or the sky may come a-falling in,
    It's all the same to the clam,
And man may sing his endless song
Of wronging rights and righting wrongs,
The clam just sets and gets along,
    It's all the same to the clam.

Shelley Silverstein

Arabella Young

Here lies, returned to clay
Miss Arabella Young,
Who on the first of May
Began to hold her tongue.

Anonymous

The Cruel Boy

There was a cruel naughty boy,
   Who sat upon the shore,
A-catching little fishes by
   The dozen and the score.

And as they squirmed and wriggled there,
   He shouted loud with glee,
'You surely cannot want to live,
   You're little-er than me.'

Just then with a malicious leer,
   And a capacious smile,
Before him from the water deep
   There rose a crocodile.

He eyed the little naughty boy,
   Then heaved a blubbering sigh,
And said, 'You cannot want to live,
   You're little-er than I.'

The fishes squirm and wriggle still,
   Beside that sandy shore,
The cruel little naughty boy,
   Was never heard of more.

Anonymous

Sammy Watkins

Young Sammy Watkins jumped out of bed;
He ran to his sister and cut off her head.
This gave his dear mother a great deal of pain;
She hopes that he never will do it again.

Anonymous

The Rabbit

The Rabbit has an evil mind,
Although he looks so good and kind.

His life is a complete disgrace,
Although he has so soft a face.

I hardly like to let you know
How far his wickedness will go.

Enough, if this poor rhyme declares
His fearful cruelty to hares.

He does his very best to keep
These gentle animals from sleep,

By joining in with noisy throngs
Of rabbits singing ribald songs.

To wake their fears and make them bound,
He simulates the Basset-hound.

And if he meets them after dark,
He imitates the greyhound's bark.

Lord Alfred Douglas

The Twins

In form and feature, face and limb,
  I grew so like my brother
That folks got taking me for him
  And each for one another.
It puzzled all our kith and kin,
  It reach'd an awful pitch;
For one of us was born a twin
  And not a soul knew which.

One day (to make the matter worse),
  Before our names were fix'd,
As we were being wash'd by nurse,
  We got completely mix'd.
And thus, you see, by Fate's decree,
  (Or rather nurse's whim),
My brother John got christen'd *me*,
  And I got christen'd *him*.

This fatal likeness even dogg'd
  My footsteps when at school,
And I was always getting flogg'd –
  For John turn'd out a fool.
I put this question hopelessly
  To every one I knew, –
What *would* you do, if you were me,
  To prove that you were *you* ?

Our close resemblance turn'd the tide
  Of my domestic life;
For somehow my intended bride
  Became my brother's wife.
In short, year after year the same
  Absurd mistakes went on;
And when I died – the neighbours came
  And buried brother John!

                    Henry Sambroke Leigh

Tarentum

There was an old man of Tarentum
Who gnashed his false teeth till he bent 'em.
    When they asked him the cost
    Of what he had lost,
He replied: 'I can't say: I just rent 'em.'

Anonymous

Montrose

There was a young man of Montrose,
Who had pockets in none of his clothes.
    When asked by his lass
    Where he carried his brass,
He said, 'Darling, I pay through the nose.'

Arnold Bennett

'Twas an Evening in November

'Twas an evening in November,
    As I very well remember,
I was strolling down the street in drunken pride,
    But my knees were all a-flutter,
    So I landed in the gutter,
And a pig came up and lay down by my side.

Yes, I lay there in the gutter,
    Thinking thoughts I could not utter,
When a colleen passing by did softly say:
    'Ye can tell a man that boozes
    By the company he chooses.'
At that the pig got up and walked away!

Anonymous

On Nevski Bridge

On Nevski Bridge a Russian stood
Chewing his beard for lack of food.
Said he, 'It's tough this stuff to eat
But a darn sight better than shredded wheat!'

Anonymous

To a Mr Wellwood Who Exaggerated

You double each story you tell,
   You double each sight that you see;
Your name's W. E. double L,
   W, double O, D.

Anonymous

Ruthless Rhymes

Billy, in one of his nice new sashes,
Fell in the fire and was burnt to ashes;
Now, although the room grows chilly,
I haven't the heart to poke poor Billy.

Auntie, did you feel no pain
   Falling from that apple-tree?
Will you do it, please, again?
   'Cos my friend here didn't see.

'There's been an accident!' they said,
'Your servant's cut in half; he's dead!'
'Indeed!' said Mr Jones, 'and please
Send me the half that's got my keys.'

Harry Graham

Spelling

I turned to the dictionary
    For a word I couldn't spell,
And closed the book when I found it
    And dipped my pen in the well.

Then I thought to myself, 'How was it ?'
    With a sense of inward pain,
And still 'twas a little doubtful,
    So I turned to the book again.

This time I remarked, 'How easy !'
    As I muttered each letter o'er,
But when I got to the inkwell
    'Twas gone, as it went before.

Then I grabbed that dictionary
    And I sped its pages through,
And under my nose I put it
    With that doubtful word in view.

I held it down with my body
    While I gripped that pen quite fast,
And I howled, as I traced each letter:
    'I've got you now, *at last*!'

Tom Masson

The Owl and the Pussy-cat

The Owl and the Pussy-cat went to sea
    In a beautiful pea-green boat,
They took some honey, and plenty of money,
    Wrapped up in a five-pound note.
The Owl looked up to the stars above,
    And sang to a small guitar,
'O lovely Pussy! O Pussy, my love,
    What a beautiful Pussy you are,
    You are,
    You are!
What a beautiful Pussy you are!'

Pussy said to the Owl, 'You elegant fowl!
   How charmingly sweet you sing!
O let us be married! too long we have tarried:
   But what shall we do for a ring?'
They sailed away, for a year and a day,
   To the land where the Bong-tree grows
And there in a wood a Piggy-wig stood
   With a ring at the end of his nose,
      His nose,
      His nose,
   With a ring at the end of his nose.

'Dear Pig, are you willing to sell for one shilling
   Your ring?' Said the Piggy, 'I will.'
So they took it away, and were married next day
   By the Turkey who lives on the hill.
They dined on mince, and slices of quince,
   Which they ate with a runcible spoon;
And hand in hand, on the edge of the sand,
   They danced by the light of the moon,
      The moon,
      The moon,
They danced by the light of the moon.

Edward Lear

The Metamorphosis of Dan Donkin, Collier

Dan Donkin was a Collier,
   A man who never smiled,
Of evil words a volleyer,
   Intemperate and wild.
But when another collier
   Fell headlong down a shaft,
The evil-minded Collier
Got ever so much jollier,
And read the works of Mollier
   – And actually laughed.

Ralph Wotherspoon

84

A Quate-So Story

A youth who wore canary spats,
The very latest thing in hats,
And on his cheeks two little mats
   Of whisker (fluff, at any rate),
Climbed languidly upon the train,
As if exhausted by the strain,
And when I said it looked like rain
   Responded 'Quate!'
Disturbed by his reply, I said
It possibly might snow instead;
He murmured 'Quate!' and turned his head
   As if he found my accents grate;
At that I ceased to be polite
And asked him frankly, 'Am I right
In thinking what you mean is "Quite"?'
   He answered 'Quate!'
I shouted, 'Do you realize
Of all the asinine replies
Yours is the worst one could devise?
   And further I should like to state
You mispronounce the wretched word,
Making it ludicrous, absurd.'
Again the awful thing occurred:
   He muttered 'Quate!'
I rose in wrath; I kicked and beat
The languid youth from head to feet
And stuffed him underneath the seat,
   And then, in tones made hoarse with hate,
I thundered, 'Are you satisfied
That it was fully time you died?'
Bloodless of face and filmy-eyed
   He whispered 'Quate!'

Anonymous

Miss James

Diana Fitzpatrick Mauleverer James
Was lucky to have the most beautiful names.
How awful for fathers and mothers to call
Their children Jemima! – or nothing at all!
But *hers* were much wiser and kinder and cleverer,
They called her Diana Fitzpatrick Mauleverer James.

A. A. Milne

Jemmy Wyatt

At rest beneath this churchyard stone
   Lies stingy JEMMY WYATT;
He died one morning just at ten, and
   Saved a dinner by it.

Anonymous

Mrs Holloway Rise

There lived an old person at Holloway Rise,
Did naught in the world but make puddings and pies;
Pies and puddings – puddings and pies –
Every fashion and form, every shape, sort, and size.
She made them of pork, beef, mutton, and eel,
As hard as a stone, and as round as a wheel.
When the children looked hungry, she ofttimes would treat 'em,
'Twould have done your heart good to have seen how they'd eat 'em.

Charles Henry Ross

Domestic Asides; or Truth in Parentheses

'I really take it very kind,
    This visit, Mrs Skinner!
I have not seen you such an age –
    (The wretch has come to dinner!)

'Your daughters, too, what loves of girls –
    What heads for painters' easels!
Come here and kiss the infant, dears –
    (And give it perhaps the measles!)

'Your charming boys I see are home
    From Reverend Mr Russell's;
'Twas very kind to bring them both –
    (What boots for my new Brussels!)

'What! little Clara left at home?
    Well now I call that shabby:
I should have loved to kiss her so –
    (A flabby, dabby, babby!)

'And Mr S., I hope he's well,
    Ah! though he lives so handy,
He never now drops in to sup –
    (The better for our brandy!)

'Come, take a seat – I long to hear
    About Matilda's marriage;
You're come of course to spend the day!
    (Thank Heaven, I hear the carriage!)

'What! must you go? next time I hope
    You'll give me longer measure;
Nay – I shall see you down the stairs –
    (With most uncommon pleasure!)

'Good-bye! good-bye! remember all,
    Next time you'll take your dinners!
(Now, David, mind I'm not at home
    In future to the Skinners!')

                            Thomas Hood

The Lion and Albert

There's a famous seaside place called Blackpool,
    That's noted for fresh air and fun,
And Mr and Mrs Ramsbottom
    Went there with young Albert, their son.

A grand little lad was young Albert,
    All dressed in his best; quite a swell
With a stick with an 'orse's 'ead 'andle,
    The finest that Woolworth's could sell.

They didn't think much to the Ocean:
    The waves, they was fiddlin' and small,
There was no wrecks and nobody drownded,
    Fact, nothing to laugh at at all.

So, seeking for further amusement,
    They paid and went into the Zoo,
Where they'd Lions and Tigers and Camels,
    And old ale and sandwiches too.

There were one great big Lion called Wallace;
    His nose were all covered with scars –
He lay in a somnolent posture
    With the side of his face on the bars.

Now Albert had heard about Lions,
    How they was ferocious and wild –
To see Wallace lying so peaceful,
    Well, it didn't seem right to the child.

So straightway the brave little feller,
    Not showing a morsel of fear,
Took his stick with its 'orse's 'ead 'andle
    And poked it in Wallace's ear.

You could see that the Lion didn't like it,
    For giving a kind of a roll,
He pulled Albert inside the cage with 'im,
    And swallowed the little lad 'ole.

Then Pa, who had seen the occurrence,
    And didn't know what to do next,
Said 'Mother! Yon Lion's 'et Albert,'
    And Mother said 'Well, I am vexed!'

Then Mr and Mrs Ramsbottom –
    Quite rightly, when all's said and done –
Complained to the Animal Keeper
    That the Lion had eaten their son.

The keeper was quite nice about it;
    He said 'What a nasty mishap.
Are you sure that it's *your* boy he's eaten?'
    Pa said 'Am I sure? There's his cap!'

The manager had to be sent for.
    He came and he said 'What's to do?'
Pa said 'Yon Lion's 'et Albert,
    And 'im in his Sunday clothes, too.'

Then Mother said, 'Right's right, young feller;
    I think it's a shame and a sin
For a lion to go and eat Albert,
    And after we've paid to come in.'

The manager wanted no trouble,
    He took out his purse right away,
Saying 'How much to settle the matter?'
    And Pa said 'What do you usually pay?'

But Mother had turned a bit awkward
    When she thought where her Albert had gone.
She said 'No! someone's got to be summonsed' –
    So that was decided upon.

Then off they went to the P'lice Station,
    In front of the Magistrate chap;
They told 'im what happened to Albert,
    And proved it by showing his cap.

The Magistrate gave his opinion
  That no one was really to blame
And he said that he hoped the Ramsbottoms
  Would have further sons to their name.

At that Mother got proper blazing,
  'And thank you, sir, kindly,' said she.
'What, waste all our lives raising children
  To feed ruddy Lions ? Not me!'

Marriott Edgar

Ceuta

There was a young fellow of Ceuta
Who rode into church on his scooter;
    He knocked down the Dean
    And said: 'Sorry, old bean,
I ought to have sounded my hooter.'

Anonymous

The Good and the Clever

If all the good people were clever,
And all clever people were good,
The world would be nicer than ever
We thought that it possibly could.

But somehow, 'tis seldom or never
The two hit it off as they should;
The good are so harsh to the clever,
The clever so rude to the good!

Elizabeth Wordsworth

Turnips

If the man who turnips cries,
Cry not when his father dies,
'Tis a proof that he had rather
Have a turnip than a father.

Samuel Johnson

The Bards

My agèd friend, Miss Wilkinson,
   Whose mother was a Lambe,
Saw Wordsworth once, and Coleridge, too,
   One morning in her p'ram'.

Birdlike the bards stooped over her –
   Like fledgling in a nest;
And Wordsworth said, 'Thou harmless babe!'
   And Coleridge was impressed.

The pretty thing gazed up and smiled,
   And softly murmured, 'Coo!'
William was then aged sixty-four
   And Samuel sixty-two.

Walter De La Mare

The Great Auk's Ghost

The Great Auk's ghost rose on one leg,
Sighed thrice and three times winkt,
And turned and poached a phantom egg
And muttered, 'I'm extinct.'

Ralph Hodgson

Three Old Men

Three old men sat a-thinking
For thirteen weeks and a day:
The first old man said nothing,
And the second old man said less,
So the third old man walked away.

Charles Henry Ross

'Biby's' Epitaph

A muvver was barfin' 'er biby one night,
The youngest of ten and a tiny young mite,
The muvver was poor and the biby was thin,
Only a skelington covered in skin;
The muvver turned rahnd for the soap off the rack,
She was but a moment, but when she turned back,
The biby was gorn; and in anguish she cried,
'Oh, where is my biby?' – The angels replied:

'Your biby 'as fell dahn the plug-'ole,
Your biby 'as gorn dahn the plug;
The poor little thing was so skinny and thin
'E oughter been barfed in a jug;
Your biby is perfeckly 'appy,
'E won't need a barf any more,
Your biby 'as fell dahn the plug-'ole,
Not lorst, but gorn before.'

Anonymous

Two Digs at Christopher Robin

Hush, hush,
Nobody cares!
Christopher Robin
Has
  Fallen
    Down –
      Stairs.

J. B. Morton

Hush, hush, whisper it not,
Christopher Robin is smoking some pot.

Alexander Macdonald

Softly the Vampire

'Softly the Vampire
   Sang to the Snail,
"You caught the Nightmare,
   I held her tail.
But while the Beetle
   Crowed on the Post,
Deep in the Greybeard
   I drowned the Ghost."'

'Greenly the Wildfire
   Opened his eyes,
Sang to the Corpse-light,
   "Come, bake the pies!
Heed not the Ghoul, love!
   Trust not his smile,
Out of the Mosque, love,
   He stole the tile."'

     Charles Godfrey Leyland

Charley Lamb

Charley Lamb, while yet a child,
   In a churchyard, on a day,
Walking with his sister mild,
   Spelling o'er the grave-stones gray, –
Seeing nought but praise, where'er
   An inscription met his eye,
Wondering, ask'd her, 'Mary, where
   Do *the wicked people* lie ?'

     Henry Sambroke Leigh

Bugs

Oh, them big bugs have bigger bugs
   That jump on 'em an' bite 'em,
An' the bigger bugs have other bugs
   An' so – *ad infinitum.*

     Will Stokes after Jonathan Swift

Rabbits

For rabbits young and rabbits old,
For rabbits hot and rabbits cold,
For rabbits tender, rabbits tough,
We thank Thee, Lord: we've had enough.

Jonathan Swift

Ancient Chinese Song

Itchy Dingle Dangle
Dingle Dangle Doo,
Going once!
Going twice!
Sold! To Fu Manchu!

Spike Milligan

The Sad Tale of Mr Mears

There was a man who had a clock,
    His name was Matthew Mears;
And every day he wound that clock
    For eight and twenty years.

And then one day he found that clock
    An eight-day clock to be;
And a madder man than Matthew Mears
    You would not wish to see.

Anonymous

Willie

Willie, with a thirst for gore,
Nailed his sister to the door.
Mother said, with humor quaint:
'Now, Willie dear, don't scratch the paint.'

Anonymous

Willie and Nell

In the family drinking well
Willie pushed his sister Nell.
She's there yet, because it kilt her –
Now we have to buy a filter.

Anonymous

John Adams

John Adams lies here, of the parish of Southwell,
A *Carrier* who *carried* his can to his mouth well;
He *carried* so much, and he *carried* so fast,
He could *carry* no more – so was *carried* at last;
For, the liquor he drank, being too much for one,
He could not *carry* off, – so he's now *carri-on*.

Lord Byron

With Every Regret

For many years the undersigned
Has struggled to improve his mind;
He now is mortified and moved
To find it is not much improved.

His unremitting efforts were
To build a sterling character;
The best that he can really claim
Is that it is about the same.

He went through many a tedious drill
Developing the power of will,
The muscles, and the memory.
They're roughly what they used to be.

Alas! the inference is plain
That Education is in vain,
And all the end of our endeavour
Is to be just as dumb as ever.

Morris Bishop

→ **Drawn Onward** ←

The learned men of Rome
Could turn a palindrome
   But they were not the first,
For Adam, says the myth,
Began conversing with
   A sentence that reversed:

→ 'Mad*am* I'm Adam' ← seemed
A phrase to be esteemed
   The moment it was popped
But that was not to be.
His lady instantly
   Said → 'Eve' ←, which left it topped.

Anonymous, that most
Prolific bard, can boast
   Of being host to this:
   → 'A man, a plan, a can-
Al, Panama!' ← What span!
   What palindromic bliss!

I've wrung the alphabet
Repeatedly to get
   A Janus-phrase as spry
At backward somersaults,
But as each hope turns false
   → In words, alas, drown I ←

Felicia Lamport

Mary

Mary had a little bear
To which she was so kind
I've often seen her bear in front –

Next!

Max Miller

98

Song

The Captain stood on his bridge alone,
　　With his telescope to his eye,
The ship she was sinking rapidly,
　　As the storm went howling by.
He saw the rush for the lifeboats,
　　And he noticed a peer old and grey,
Then a sailor approached and saluted,
　　And thus to the peer he did say:

Chorus:

Pray take my place in the lifeboat,
　　'Tis a gesture I willingly make,
Since I fagged for your nephew at Repton,
　　It's the least I might do for his sake.
And when next, sir, you're seeing your nephew,
　　Pray sing him this short refrain:
'Piddock minor went down like a Repton man,
　　And gladly he'd do it again.'

J. B. Morton

The Matron's Message

We have patients in the home
None of whom are fit to roam,
And what is more important still,
Each must pay his weekly bill.

Nathaniel Gubbins

The Misses B.

Miss Buss and Miss Beale
Cupid's darts do not feel.
How different from us
Miss Beale and Miss Buss.

Anonymous

The Gardener

It was the busy hour of 4
When from a city hardware store
Emerged a gentleman who bore
    1 hoe,
    1 spade,
    1 wheelbarrow.
From there our hero promptly went
Into a seed establishment
And for these things his money spent:
    1 peck of bulbs,
    1 job lot of shrubs,
    1 quart assorted seeds.
He has a garden under way
And if he's fairly lucky, say,
He'll have about the last of May
    1 privet bush,
    1 ivy plant,
    1 radish.

Anonymous

Bingo

The Brewer's dog leapt over the style,
and his name was Little Bingo:
B with an I, I with an N,
N with a G, G with an O,
they called him Little Bingo!

This Brewer, Sir, he brewed good ale,
and he called it Super Stingo:
S with a T, I with an N,
N with a G, G with an O.
he called it Super Stingo!

Now is this not a pretty song?
Of course it is, by Jingo,
 J with an I, I with an N,
N with a G, G with an O
Stingo! Jingo! Bingo!

Anonymous

Not so Gorgeous

Dorothy's drawers are creamy gauze;
   Lil's are long and slack;
Tonia's tights are crocheted whites;
   Jennifer Jane's are black.

Betty's bloomers are slaty grey,
   And she tucks her skirt inside;
Polly's are pink – since yesterday –
   I think she's had them dyed.

Sarah's silks were awf'ly dear –
   The best her mum could get;
And (may I whisper it in your ear?)
   Nancy's knickers are wet!

Sue's are blue, and Prue's are too,
   And little Pam's are sweet;
While naughty Meg has lost a leg,
   And Tilly has torn her seat.

Swanky Maisie's are trimmed with daisies
   And patched with coloured stuffs;
But those on Milly look awful silly –
   They sort of flap their cuffs!

Jill's have frills, and Pat's are plain,
   With a button in case they fall;
And (may I whisper once again?)
   I HAVEN'T A PAIR AT ALL!

J. A. Lindon

Kent

There was a young woman from Kent
Who said that she knew what it meant
   When men asked her to dine
   Upon oyster with wine –
She knew, O, she knew, and she went!

Anonymous

A Riddle

Because I am by Nature *blind*,
I wisely chuse to walk *behind*;
However, to avoid Disgrace,
I let no Creature see my *Face*.
My *Words* are few, but spoke with *Sense*:
And yet my *speaking* gives Offence:
Or, if to *whisper* I presume,
The Company will fly the Room.
By all the World I am *oppress't*,
And my *Oppression* gives them *Rest*.

Jonathan Swift

Answer: Bum.

A Dream

I dreamed a dream next Tuesday week,
    Beneath the apple-trees;
I thought my eyes were big pork-pies,
    And my nose was Stilton cheese.
The clock struck twenty minutes to six,
    When a frog sat on my knee;
I asked him to lend me eighteenpence
    But he borrowed a shilling of me.

Anonymous

Matilda

Who told Lies, and was Burned to Death

Matilda told such dreadful lies,
It made one gasp and stretch one's eyes;
Her Aunt, who, from her earliest youth,
Had kept a strict regard for truth,
Attempted to believe Matilda:
The effort very nearly killed her,
And would have done so, had not she
Discovered this infirmity.
For once, towards the close of day,

102

Matilda, growing tired of play,
And finding she was left alone,
Went tiptoe to the telephone
And summoned the immediate aid
Of London's noble fire-brigade.
Within an hour the gallant band
Were pouring in on every hand,
From Putney, Hackney Downs, and Bow
With courage high and hearts a-glow
They galloped, roaring through the town,
'Matilda's house is burning down!'
Inspired by British cheers and loud
Proceeding from the frenzied crowd,
They ran their ladders through a score
Of windows on the ballroom floor;
And took peculiar pains to souse
The pictures up and down the house,
Until Matilda's Aunt succeeded
In showing them they were not needed;
And even then she had to pay
To get the men to go away!

It happened that a few weeks later
Her Aunt was off to the theatre
To see that interesting play
The Second Mrs Tanqueray,
She had refused to take her niece
To hear this entertaining piece:
A deprivation just and wise
To punish her for telling lies.
That night a fire *did* break out –
You should have heard Matilda shout!
You should have heard her scream and bawl,
And throw the window up and call
To people passing in the street –
(The rapidly increasing heat
Encouraging her to obtain
Their confidence) – but all in vain!
For every time she shouted 'Fire!'
They only answered 'Little liar!'
And therefore when her Aunt returned,
Matilda, and the house, were burned.

                                        Hilaire Belloc

Holy Smoke

I am the Vicar of St Paul's
And I'm ringing the steeple bell,
The floor of the church is on fire,
Or the lid has come off hell.

Shall I ring the fire brigade?
Or should I trust in the Lord?
Oh dear! I've just remembered,
I don't think we're insured!

'What's this then?' said the fire chief.
'Is this church C of E?
It is? Then we can't put it out,
My lads are all R.C.!'

Spike Milligan

The Pig

The pig, if I am not mistaken,
Supplies us sausage, ham, and bacon.
Let others say his heart is big –
I call it stupid of the pig.

Ogden Nash

Ryde

There was a young lady of Ryde
Who ate a green apple and died;
    The apple fermented
    Inside the lamented,
And made cider inside her inside.

Anonymous

Lyme

There once was a person from Lyme
Who married three wives at a time.
    When asked, 'Why a third?'
    He replied, 'One's absurd,
And bigamy, sir, is a crime.'

Anonymous

Sir Christopher Wren

Sir Christopher Wren
Said, 'I am going to dine with some men.
'If anybody calls
'Say I am designing St Paul's.'

E. C. Bentley

Miss Ellen Gee of Kew

Peerless yet hopeless maid of Q,
  Accomplish'd L N G;
Never again shall I and U
  Together sip our T.

For oh! the fates, I know not Y,
  Sent 'midst the flowers a B;
Which ven'mous stung her in the I,
  So that she could not C.

L N exclaimed, 'Vile spiteful B,
  If ever I catch U
On jessmine, rosebud or sweet P,
  I'll change your singing Q.

'I'll send you like a lamb or U,
  Across the Atlantic C;
From our delightful village Q,
  To distant O Y E.

A stream runs from my wounded I,
  Salt as the briny C,
As rapid as the X or Y,
  The O I O or D.

'Then fare thee ill, insensate B,
  Which stung nor yet knew Y,
Since not for wealthy Durham's C
  Would I have lost my I.'

They bear with tears poor L N G
  In funeral R A,
A clay cold corse now doomed to B,
  Whilst I mourn her D K.

Ye nymphs of Q, then shun each B,
  List to the reason Y;
For should A B C U at T,
  He'll surely sting your I.

Now in a grave L deep in Q,
  She's cold as cold can B;
Whilst robins sing upon A U,
  Her dirge and L E G.

            Anonymous

The Man Who Discovered the Use of a Chair

The man who discovered the use of a chair,
  Odds-bobs –
          What a wonderful man!
He used to sit down on it, tearing his hair,
  Till he thought of a highly original plan.

For years he had sat on his chair, like you,
  Quite-still!
          But his looks were grim,
For he wished to be famous (as great men do),
  And nobody ever would listen to him.

Now he went one night to a dinner of state,
  Hear! hear!
          In the proud Guildhall!
And he sat on his chair, and he ate from a plate,
  But nobody heard his opinions at all;

There were ten fat aldermen down for a speech,
  (*Grouse! Grouse!*
          What a dreary bird!)
With five fair minutes allotted to each,
  But never a moment for *him* to be heard.

But each being ready to talk, I suppose,
  Order! Order!
          They cried, *for the Chair!*
And, much to their wonder, our friend arose
  And fastened his eye on the eye of the Mayor.

'We have come,' he said, 'to the fourteenth course!
   High-time,
                For the Chair,' he said.
Then, with both of his hands, and with all of his force,
   He hurled his chair at the Lord Mayor's head.

It missed that head with the width of a hair.
   Gee-whizz!
              What a horrible squeak!
But it crashed through the big bay-window there
   And smashed a bus into Wednesday week.

And the very next day, in the dignified *Times*
   (*Great-Guns!*
              How the headlines ran!)
In spite of the kings and the wars and the crimes,
   There was nearly a column about that man.

Envoi

Oh, if you get dizzy when authors write
   (*My stars!*
              And you very well may!)
That white is black and that black is white,
   You should sit, quite still, in your chair and say:

It is easy enough to be famous now
   (*Puff-puff*
              How the trumpets blare!),
Provided, of course, that you don't care how,
   Like the man who discovered the use of a chair.

                          Alfred Noyes

A Ballade of
The Genial Holiday Maker

In Brighton there's a German band,
At Folkestone there are dismal leas,
Skegness is bracing, Barmouth bland,
And Whitby full of foul disease:
Portrush, 'tis said, has failed to please.
For Ramsgate there be few that care.
At Dover you may take your ease –
But don't try Weston-super-Mare.

Shoreham is loathlier than the Strand.
At Blackpool one is stung with bees,
At Douglas crimes are daily planned,
At Weymouth they won't let you sneeze.
Birchington smells like mouldy cheese,
And Bude is barren, bleak and bare,
At Filey you are like to freeze –
But don't try Weston-super-Mare.

Sprawl if you will on Margate sand;
At Tenby gorge on trippers' teas;
Motor from Rottingdean to Rand;
Crawl through Clovelly on your knees;
Be sick on Sidmouth's heaving seas;
Be wheeled through Bournemouth in a chair;
Be blown about by Bognor's breeze –
But don't try Weston-super-Mare.

Envoi

Prince, Felixstowe may teem with fleas,
And Yarmouth's bloaters taint the air –
Content yourself with all of these –
But don't try Weston-super-Mare.

T. Michael Pope

The Jam Fish

A Jam Fish sat on a hard-bake rock,
   His head in his left hand fin,
He was knitting his wife a sky-blue sock
   With a second-hand rolling pin.
His wife was watching her old Aunt Brill
   Sew acid drops on to his shirt,
While his grandmother fitted a caramel frill
   To a Butterscotch tartan skirt.

His cousin Jelly Fish gently swam
   In a pool of parsley sauce,
While the Jam Fish sighed, 'I am only Jam,
   And must wait for the second course.
When the rice mould quivers on the dish,
   And shakes at the children's sneers,
Till the scented voice of the old Jam Fish
   Shall melt their scorn to tears.'

Edward Abbott Parry

School Report

'Too easily satisfied. Spelling still poor.
   Her grammar's erratic. Lacks care.
Would succeed if she worked. Inclined to be smug.'
   I think that's a wee bit unfare.

Ah well, their it is! Disappointing perhaps,
   For a mum what has always had brane,
But we can't all have looks or be good at our books . . .
   She's her father all over agane.

Carole Paine

A Brilliant Idea

An old woman at Tarranginnie
Took her son who was frightfully skinny
   To the local M.D.
   Who said, 'Let me see,
Feed him up a bit, Ma'am, half-a-guinea.'

Shaw Neilson

The Sleeping-bag

On the outside grows the furside, on the inside grows the skinside;
So the furside is the outside, and the skinside is the inside.
As the skinside is the inside, and the furside is the outside;
One 'side' likes the skinside inside, and the furside on the outside.
Others like the skinside outside, and the furside on the inside;
As the skinside is the hardside, and the furside is the soft side.
If you turn the skinside outside, thinking you will side with that 'side,'
Then the soft side, furside's inside, which some argue is the wrong
    side.
If you turn the furside outside, as you say it grows on that side;
Then your outside's next the skinside, which for comfort's not the
    right side:
For the skinside is the cold side, and your outside's not your warm
    side;
And two cold sides coming side by side are not right sides one 'side'
    decides.
If you decide to side with that 'side,' turn the outside, furside, inside;
Then the hard side, cold side, skinside's, beyond all question, inside
    outside.

H. G. Ponting

The Giraffe

A doubtful friend is the Giraffe,
Distrust him when you hear him laugh.

He laughs like people at a ball,
And not because he's pleased at all.

He stretches out his neck like tape,
Until its length precludes escape.

And then he dexterously throws
The window open with his nose.

And if you hide beneath a chair
He finds you out, and pins you there.

George Wyndham

The Crinoline

In days
long gone
our grandmas
quaint   Set
all the world
a-grin   By
donning
when   they
wore   their
paint, The   bulky
crinoline.   They
waddled in the park and
town   Like   portions   of
balloons, Or monster egg-
cups upside down. Or cut-in-
two cocoons; They blocked the
roadway and the lane, Their bulki-
ness was such; Likewise they distant kept a swain Who strove a waist
to clutch. They whirled about in every
breeze And wobbled in the gale, Till
timid men went on their knees In apprehen-
sion pale. In play-house or in con-
cert-hall, In vestibule or stair, They
pushed the males towards the wall And kept
them tightly there. The drawing-room they
crammed and jammed; They blocked the cab and
'bus. Until the public loudly damned Their
plaguey overplus; And while the curs-ed crinoline The heart of mankind vexed, A voice arose
from out the din "What next ? O, Lord, what next ?"

E. G. Murphy

Ecstasy

Neptune loves the breast-stroke
  As Margaret loves the sea,
And now it is his best joke
  To keep her from her tea;

While mother bakes in dudgeon
  Beneath the hot sea-wall,
And sees her do the trudgen,
  And sees her do the crawl,

Neptune smoothes each contour,
  Each long elastic leg,
With not a soul *à l'entour*
  Embraces blooming Meg;

As supple as a porpoise
  She welcomes his advances –
Ah, Neptune, *habeas corpus*!
  The gods have all the chances.
                    William Plomer

The Cure

'I've swallowed a fly,' cried Marjorie Fry.
  (We could hear it buzzing inside her.)
'And I haven't a hope of getting it out
  Unless I swallow a spider.'

We found a web by the garden wall,
  And back to the house we hurried
And offered the spider to Marjorie Fry,
  Who was looking extremely worried.

'Now shut your eyelids, Marjorie Fry,
  And open your wee mouth wider.
Whatever it does, the fly won't buzz
  If only you'll swallow the spider.'

                    Alfred Noyes

The Man in the Moon

And The Man in the Moon has a boil on his ear –
  Whee!
    Whing!
      What a singular thing!
I know! but these facts are authentic, my dear, –
There's a boil on his ear; and a corn on his chin –
He calls it a dimple – but dimples stick in –
Yet it might be a dimple turned over, you know!
  Whang!
    Ho!
      Why, certainly so!
It might be a dimple turned over, you know!

And The Man in the Moon has a rheumatic knee –
  Gee!
    Whizz!
      What a pity that is!
And his toes have worked round where his heels ought to be. –
So whenever he wants to go North he goes *South*,
And comes back with porridge-crumbs all round his mouth
And he brushes them off with a Japanese fan,
  Whing!
    Whann!
      What a marvellous man!
What a very remarkably marvellous man!

And The Man in the Moon, sighed The Raggedy Man,
  Gits!
    So!
      Sullonsome, you know!, –
Up there by hisse'f sence creation began! –
That when I call on him and then come away,
He grabs me and holds me and begs me to stay, –
Till – *Well!* if it wasn't fer *Jimmy-cum-jim*,
  Dadd!
    Limb!
      I'd go pardners with him –
Jes jump my job here and be pardners with *him!*

                                        J. W. Riley

The Yarn of the 'Nancy Bell'

'Twas on the shores that round our coast
   From Deal to Ramsgate span,
That I found alone on a piece of stone
   An elderly naval man.

His hair was weedy, his beard was long,
   And weedy and long was he,
And I heard this wight on the shore recite,
   In a singular minor key:

'Oh, I am a cook and a captain bold,
   And the mate of the *Nancy* brig,
And a bo'sun tight, and a midshipmite,
   And the crew of the captain's gig.'

And he shook his fists and he tore his hair,
   Till I really felt afraid,
For I couldn't help thinking the man had been drinking,
   And so I simply said:

'Oh, elderly man, it's little I know
   Of the duties of men of the sea,
But I'll eat my hand if I understand
   How you can possibly be

'At once a cook, and a captain bold,
   And the mate of the *Nancy* brig,
And a bo'sun tight, and a midshipmite,
   And the crew of the captain's gig.'

Then he gave a hitch to his trousers, which
   Is a trick all seamen larn,
And having got rid of a thumping quid,
   He spun this painful yarn:

''Twas in the good ship *Nancy Bell*
   That we sailed to the Indian sea,
And there on a reef we come to grief,
   Which has often occurred to me.

'And pretty nigh all o' the crew was drowned
   (There was seventy-seven o' soul),
And only ten of the *Nancy*'s men
   Said "Here!" to the muster-roll.

'There was me and the cook and the captain bold,
   And the mate of the *Nancy* brig,
And the bo'sun tight, and a midshipmite,
   And the crew of the captain's gig.

'For a month we'd neither wittles nor drink,
   Till a-hungry we did feel,
So we drawed a lot, and accordin' shot
   The captain for our meal.

'The next lot fell to the *Nancy*'s mate,
   And a delicate dish he made;
Then our appetite with the midshipmite
   We seven survivors stayed.

'And then we murdered the bo'sun tight,
   And he much resembled pig;
Then we wittled free, did the cook and me,
   On the crew of the captain's gig.

'Then only the cook and me was left,
   And the delicate question, "Which
Of us two goes to the kettle?" arose
   And we argued it out as sich.

'For I loved that cook as a brother, I did,
   And the cook he worshipped me;
But we'd both be blowed if we'd either be stowed
   In the other chap's hold, you see.

'"I'll be eat if you dines off me," says Tom,
   "Yes, that," says I, "you'll be," –
"I'm boiled if I die, my friend," quoth I,
   And "Exactly so," quoth he.

'Says he, "Dear James, to murder me
    Were a foolish thing to do,
For don't you see that you can't cook *me*,
    While I can – and will – cook *you!*"'

'So he boils the water, and takes the salt
    And the pepper in portions true
(Which he never forgot), and some chopped shalot,
    And some sage and parsley too.

'"Come here," says he, with a proper pride,
    Which his smiling features tell,
"'Twill soothing be if I let you see,
    How extremely nice you'll smell."

'And he stirred it round and round and round,
    And he sniffed at the foaming froth;
When I ups with his heels, and smothers his squeals
    In the scum of the boiling broth.

'And I eat that cook in a week or less,
    And – as I eating be
The last of his chops, why, I almost drops,
    For a wessel in sight I see!

'And I never grieve, and I never smile,
    And I never larf nor play,
But I sit and croak, and a single joke
    I have – which is to say:

'Oh, I am a cook and a captain bold,
    And the mate of the *Nancy* brig,
And a bo'sun tight, and a midshipmite,
    And the crew of the captain's gig!'

                        Sir William Schwenk Gilbert

Mispronounced Limerick

If-itty-teshi-mow Jays
Haddee ny up-plo-now-shi-buh nays;
    He lote im aw dow,
    Witty motti-fy flow;
A-flew-ty ho-lot-itty flays!

The Same Limerick correctly pronounced

Infinitesimal James
Had nine unpronounceable names;
    He wrote them all down,
    With a mortified frown,
And threw the whole lot in the flames.

Anonymous

The Blind Men and the Elephant

It was six men of Indostan,
    To learning much inclined,
Who went to see the Elephant
    (Though all of them were blind),
That each by observation
    Might satisfy his mind.

The First approached the Elephant,
    And, happening to fall
Against his broad and sturdy side,
    At once began to bawl,
'God bless me! but the Elephant
    Is very like a wall!'

The Second, feeling of the tusk,
  Cried – 'Ho! what have we here
So very round and smooth, and sharp?
  To me 'tis mighty clear
This wonder of an Elephant
  Is very like a spear!'

The Third approached the animal
  And happening to take
The squirming trunk within his hands,
  Thus boldly up and spake:
'I see' – quoth he – 'the Elephant
  Is very like a snake!'

The Fourth reached out his eager hand
  And felt about the knee:
'What most this wondrous beast is like
  Is mighty plain' – quoth he –
''Tis clear enough the Elephant
  Is very like a tree!'

The Fifth, who chanced to touch the ear,
  Said – 'E'en the blindest man
Can tell what this resembles most;
  Defy the fact who can,
This marvel of an Elephant
  Is very like a fan!'

The Sixth no sooner had begun
  About the beast to grope,
Than, seizing on the swinging tail
  That fell within his scope,
'I see' – quoth he – 'the Elephant
  Is very like a rope!'

And so these men of Indostan
  Disputed loud and long,
Each in his own opinion
  Exceeding stiff and strong,
Though each was partly in the right,
  And all were in the wrong!

                    John G. Saxe

Croft

Aloft,
In the loft,
Sits Croft;
He is soft.

Stevie Smith

The Song of Robinson Crusoe

The night was thick and hazy
When the 'Piccadilly Daisy'
Carried down the crew and captain in the sea;
And I think the water drowned 'em;
For they never, never found 'em,
And I know they didn't come ashore with me.

Oh! 'twas very sad and lonely
When I found myself the only
Population on this cultivated shore;
But I've made a little tavern
In a rocky little cavern,
And I sit and watch for people at the door.

I spent no time in looking
For a girl to do my cooking,
As I'm quite a clever hand at making stews:
But I had that fellow Friday,
Just to keep the tavern tidy,
And to put a Sunday polish on my shoes.

I have a little garden
That I'm cultivating lard in,
As the things I eat are rather tough and dry;
For I live on toasted lizards,
Prickly pears, and parrot gizzards,
And I'm really very fond of beetle-pie.

The clothes I had were furry,
And it made me fret and worry
When I found the moths were eating off the hair;
And I had to scrape and sand 'em,
And I boiled 'em and I tanned 'em,
Till I got the fine morocco suit I wear.

I sometimes seek diversion
In a family excursion
With the few domestic animals you see;
And we take along a carrot
As refreshment for the parrot,
And a little can of jungleberry tea.

Then we gather, as we travel,
Bits of moss and dirty gravel,
And we chip off little specimens of stone;
And we carry home as prizes
Funny bugs, of handy sizes,
Just to give the day a scientific tone.

If the roads are wet and muddy
We remain at home and study, –
For the Goat is very clever at a sum, –
And the Dog, instead of fighting,
Studies ornamental writing,
While the Cat is taking lessons on the drum.

Charles Edward Carryl

The Hen

No bird can sing so sweetly
        As the Hen;
No bird can walk so neatly,
        And again,
    Apart from being beautiful,
    I know no bird so dutiful,
For it lays an egg discreetly –
        Now and then.

How nice, when dawn is bringing
        In the day,
To wake and hear it singing
        O'er it's *lay*.
    Ah yes! how good the Hen is,
    So save up all your pennies,
And buy one (one with trousers) –
        It will pay.

John Joy Bell

The Sorcerer's Song

Oh! my name is John Wellington Wells –
I'm a dealer in magic and spells,
In blessings and curses,
And ever-filled purses,
In prophecies, witches, and knells!
If you want a proud foe to 'make tracks' –
If you'd melt a rich uncle in wax –
You've but to look in
On our resident Djinn,
Number seventy, Simmery Axe.

We've a first-class assortment of magic;
And for raising a posthumous shade
With effects that are comic or tragic,
There's no cheaper house in the trade.
Love-philtre – we've quantities of it;
And for knowledge if any one burns,
We keep an extremely small prophet, a prophet
Who brings us unbounded returns:
For he can prophesy
With a wink *of* his eye,
Peep with security
Into futurity,
Sum up your history,
Clear up a mystery,
Humour proclivity
For a nativity.
With mirrors so magical,
Tetrapods tragical,
Bogies spectacular,
Answers oracular,
Facts astronomical,
Solemn or comical,
And, if you want it, he
Makes a reduction on taking a quantity!
Oh!
If any one anything lacks,
He'll find it all ready in stacks,
If he'll only look in
On the resident Djinn,
Number seventy, Simmery Axe!

He can raise you hosts,
         Of ghosts,
And that without reflectors;
  And creepy things
         With wings,
And gaunt and grisly spectres!
  He can fill you crowds
         Of shrouds,
And horrify you vastly;
  He can rack your brains
         With chains,
And gibberings grim and ghastly.
  Then, if you plan it, he
  Changes organity,
  With an urbanity,
  Full of Satanity,
  Vexes humanity
  With an inanity
  Fatal to vanity –
Driving your foes to the verge of insanity.
  Barring tautology,
  In demonology,
  'Lectro biology,
  Mystic nosology,
  Spirit philology,
  High class astrology,
  Such is his knowledge, he
Isn't the man to require an apology!
         Oh!
My name is John Wellington Wells,
I'm a dealer in magic and spells,
  In blessings and curses,
  And ever-filled purses –
In prophecies, witches, and knells.
If any one anything lacks,
He'll find it all ready in stacks,
  If he'll only look in
  On the resident Djinn,
Number seventy, Simmery Axe!

Sir William Schwenk Gilbert

When Father Carves the Duck

We all look on with anxious eyes
   When father carves the duck,
And mother almost always sighs
   When father carves the duck;
Then all of us prepare to rise,
And hold our bibs before our eyes,
And be prepared for some surprise,
   When father carves the duck.

He braces up and grabs a fork
   Whene'er he carves a duck,
And won't allow a soul to talk
   Until he's carved the duck.
The fork is jabbed into the sides,
Across the breast the knife he slides,
While every careful person hides
   From flying chips of duck.

The platter's always sure to slip
   When father carves a duck,
And how it makes the dishes skip!
   Potatoes fly amuck!
The squash and cabbage leap in space,
We get some gravy in our face,
And father mutters Hindoo grace
   Whene'er he carves a duck.

We then have learned to walk around
   The dining-room and pluck
From off the window-sills and walls
   Our share of father's duck.
While father growls and blows and jaws
And swears the knife was full of flaws,
And mother laughs at him because
   He couldn't carve a duck.

              E. V. Wright

The Frog

Be kind and tender to the Frog,
　　And do not call him names,
As 'Slimy skin', or 'Polly-wog',
　　Or likewise 'Ugly James',
Or 'Gape-a-grin', or 'Toad-gone-wrong',
　　Or 'Billy Bandy-knees':
The Frog is justly sensitive
　　To epithets like these.
No animal will more repay
　　A treatment kind and fair;
At least so lonely people say
Who keep a frog (and, by the way,
　　They are extremely rare).

Hilaire Belloc

Word of Honour

No power of language can express
The irritation and distress
    It used to be to Mrs Trales
    To see her children bite their nails.

In vain she tied their hands in bags:
They chewed the corners into rags.
    Even bitter aloes proved a waste:
    The children grew to like the taste.

So for a week with constant smacks
She bound their hands behind their backs:
    Then said, 'Now promise, George and Jane,
    Never to bite your nails again!'

And when the promise had been wrung
From sobbing throat and stammering tongue,
    She added, with a threatening brow,
    'Mind! You're upon your honour now!'

The votive pair, their spirits bowed,
With sullen looks the claim allowed;
    And 'bound in honour' forth they went
    To try a fresh experiment.

Time passed: till Mrs Trales one day
Remarked in quite a casual way –
    Threading her needle in between –
    'Come, show me if your hands are clean!'

With conscious looks the guilty pair
    Adjusted flattened palms in air:
    But she, not meaning to be lax,
    Observed, 'Now let me see the backs!'

Which being shown, there plain to see
Were nails as short as short could be!
    'What!' cried Mamma, her anger stirred,
    'Is this the way you keep your word?'

Then, nerved to desperation, Jane
Cried, 'Wait, Mamma, and I'll explain:
    For bad at first though things appear,
    Indeed it is not as you fear!

'Though at first glance our nails may strike
Your eye as shorter than you'd like,
    Yet, dear Mamma, pray bear in mind
    For weeks they have been much behind!

'And often, when the wish occurred
To bite them, we recalled our word,
    And never, never would we break
    The promise we were forced to make!

'So, now, whenever George or I
Starve for a taste of finger-pie,
    Then turn and turn about we dine –
    First I bite his, then he bites mine.'

What happened next you may surmise,
While in between came anguished cries –
    'You never did put me or Brother
    On honour not to bite each other!'

Laurence Houseman

A Reasonable Affliction

On his death-bed poor Lubin lies;
    His spouse is in despair;
With frequent sobs and mutual cries,
    They both express their care.

'A different cause,' says Parson Sly,
    'The same effect may give:
Poor Lubin fears that he may die;
    His wife, that he may live.'

Matthew Prior

The Lobster Quadrille

'Will you walk a little faster?' said a whiting to a snail.
'There's a porpoise close behind us, and he's treading on my tail.
See how eagerly the lobsters and the turtles all advance!
They are waiting on the shingle – will you come and join the dance?
  Will you, won't you, will you, won't you, will you join the
   dance?
  Will you, won't you, will you, won't you, won't you join the
   dance?

'You can really have no notion how delightful it will be,
When they take us up and throw us, with the lobsters, out to sea!'
But the snail replied 'Too far, too far!' and gave a look askance –
Said he thanked the whiting kindly, but he would not join the dance.
  Would not, could not, would not, could not, would not join the
   dance.
  Would not, could not, would not, could not, could not join the
   dance.

'What matters it how far we go?' his scaly friend replied.
'There is another shore, you know, upon the other side.
The further off from England the nearer is to France –
Then turn not pale, beloved snail, but come and join the dance.
  Will you, won't you, will you, won't you, will you join the
   dance?
  Will you, won't you, will you, won't you, won't you join the
   dance?'

Lewis Carroll

Motto for a Sundial

I am a sundial, and I make a botch
Of what is done far better by a watch.

Hilaire Belloc

The Auk

The Auk possessed such awkward legs,
   Such very awkward legs, it
Grew tired of sitting on its eggs,
   And so it made its exit.

Yet, some assert its sad death might
   Be due to trade not paying:
Thus, seeing prospects far from bright,
   The Auk abandoned laying.

In any case the egg's so rare,
   You hardly ever meet it.
But should you find one anywhere,
   For goodness' sake don't eat it!

John Joy Bell

Of Pygmies, Palms and Pirates

Of pygmies, palms and pirates,
Of islands and lagoons,
Of blood-bespotted frigates,
Of crags and octoroons,
Of whales and broken bottles,
Of quicksands cold and grey,
Of ullages and dottles,
I have no more to say.

Of barley, corn and furrows,
Of farms and turf that heaves
Above such ghostly burrows
As twitch on summer eves
Of fallow-land and pasture,
Of skies both pink and grey,
I made a statement last year
And have no more to say.

Mervyn Peake

My Name and I

The impartial Law enrolled a name
   For my especial use:
My rights in it would rest the same
Whether I puffed it into fame
   Or sank it in abuse.

Robert was what my parents guessed
   When first they peered at me,
And *Graves* an honourable bequest
With Georgian silver and the rest
   From my male ancestry.

They taught me: 'You are *Robert Graves*
   (Which you must learn to spell),
But see that *Robert Graves* behaves,
Whether with honest men or knaves,
   Exemplarily well.'

Then though my I was always I,
   Illegal and unknown,
With nothing to arrest it by –
As will be obvious when I die
   And *Robert Graves* lives on –

I cannot well repudiate
   This noun, this natal star,
This gentlemanly self, this mate
So kindly forced on me by fate,
   Time and the registrar;

And therefore hurry him ahead
   As an ambassador
To fetch me home my beer and bread
Or commandeer the best green bed,
   As he has done before.

Yet, understand, I am not he
   Either in mind or limb;
My name will take less thought for me,
In worlds of men I cannot see,
   Than ever I for him.

                    Robert Graves

Jemima

There was a little girl, she wore a little hood,
    And a curl down the middle of her forehead,
When she was good, she was very, very good,
    But when she was bad, she was horrid.

One day she went upstairs, while her parents, unawares,
    In the kitchen down below were occupied with meals,
And she stood upon her head, on her little truckle-bed,
    And she then began hurraying with her heels.

Her mother heard the noise, and thought it was the boys,
    A-playing at a combat in the attic,
But when she climbed the stair and saw Jemima there,
    She took and she did whip her most emphatic!

Anonymous

The Duck

Behold the duck.
It does not cluck.
A cluck it lacks.
It quacks.
It is specially fond
Of a puddle or pond.
When it dines or sups,
It bottoms ups.

Ogden Nash

There Was an Old Party

There was an old party who smelt at a rose,
And a crickelty-crackle ran right up his nose,
Danced a jig in his head, and, before he could wince,
Flew out at his ear, and has not been seen since.

Charles Henry Ross

The Zebra

The Zebra, born both black and white,
Is just the jungle clown.
The lionesses hunt him up,
The lions hunt him down.
His life, in consequence, is brief
And seems inclined to end in grief.
And so you see, between the two,
He's more contented in the zoo.

Roland Young

The Cook Cooked

A hare, who long had hung for dead,
    But *really* brew'd sedition,
Once set a scheme on foot, and said,
She could not take it in her head,
    That *hares* should be nutrition;

A turkey next began to speak,
    But said her task was harder,
Because the cook had tucked her beak
Behind her wing, for half a week
    That she'd been in the larder.

At length, with some ado she said,
    That as for her opinion,
If any prudent plan were laid,
Her latest drop of blood should aid,
    To rescue the dominion.

A murmur more than usual grave,
    Then issued from an oyster,
Who moaning through a broken stave,
Full many a doleful reason gave,
    Against his wooden cloister.

134

Eels, sliding on a marble shelf,
    The growing treason aided;
And e'en a turtle 'woke itself,
To reprobate the cruel pelf,
    In callepash that traded.

So hand and foot, and fin and paw,
    In mutual faith were shaken;
And all the patriots made a law,
To murder every cook they saw,
    The moment he was taken.

Ere long a wretched wight was found,
    And carried to the kitchen;
The traitor of a jack went round;
The turkey dredg'd, the cook was brown'd,
And chanticleer the banquet crown'd,
    With songs the most bewitching.

Anne Taylor

Relativity

There was a young lady named Bright,
Who travelled much faster than light,
    She started one day
    In the relative way,
And returned on the previous night.

Anonymous

A Young Man of Egypt

A young man in Egypt invented a trap,
But caught his own nose, in the midst of a nap;
And the worst of it was, to the trap that you see,
This clever young man had not yet made a key.

Charles Henry Ross

The Duke of Plaza-Toro

In enterprise of martial kind,
   When there was any fighting,
He led his regiment from behind
   (He found it less exciting).
But when away his regiment ran,
   His place was at the fore, O –
     That celebrated,
     Cultivated,
     Underrated
      Nobleman,
   The Duke of Plaza-Toro!
In the first and foremost flight, ha, ha!
You always found that knight, ha, ha!
     That celebrated,
     Cultivated,
     Underrated
      Nobleman,
   The Duke of Plaza-Toro!

When, to evade Destruction's hand,
   To hide they all proceeded,
No soldier in that gallant band
   Hid half as well as he did.
He lay concealed throughout the war,
   And so preserved his gore, O!
     That unaffected,
     Undetected,
     Well connected
      Warrior,
   The Duke of Plaza-Toro!
In every doughty deed, ha, ha!
He always took the lead, ha, ha!
     That unaffected,
     Undetected,
     Well connected
      Warrior,
   The Duke of Plaza-Toro!

When told that they would all be shot
    Unless they left the service,
    That hero hesitated not,
    So marvellous his nerve is.
He sent his resignation in,
    The first of all his corps, O!
        That very knowing,
        Overflowing,
        Easy-going
            Paladin,
    The Duke of Plaza-Toro!
To men of grosser clay, ha, ha!
He always showed the way, ha, ha!
    That very knowing,
    Overflowing,
    Easy-going
        Paladin,
The Duke of Plaza-Toro!

Sir William Schwenk Gilbert

The Shrimp

I'm a shrimp! I'm a shrimp! Of diminutive size.
Inspect my antennae, and look at my eyes;
I'm a natural syphon, when dipped in a cup,
For I drain the contents to the latest drop up.
I care not for craw-fish, I heed not the prawn,
From a flavour especial my fame has been drawn;
Nor e'en to the crab or the lobster do yield,
When I'm properly cook'd and efficiently peeled.
Quick! quick! pile the coals – let your saucepan be deep,
For the weather is warm, and I'm sure not to keep;
Off, off with my head – split my shell into three –
I'm a shrimp! I'm a shrimp – to be eaten with tea.

Robert Barnabas Brough

A Warning

What became of tyrannical Pat,
Who pelted the dog, and beat the cat ?
Why, Puss scratched his face, and tore his hat,
And Dash knocked him over as flat as a mat,
        Mind that!

Robert Barnabas Brough

Hunter Trials

It's awf'lly bad luck on Diana,
   Her ponies have swallowed their bits;
She fished down their throats with a spanner
   And frightened them all into fits.

And now she's attempting to borrow.
   Do lend her some bits, Mummy, *do*;
I'll lend her my own for tomorrow,
   But today I'll be wanting them too.

Just look at Prunella on Guzzle,
   The wizardest pony on earth;
Why doesn't she slacken his muzzle
   And tighten the breech in his girth ?

I say, Mummy, there's Mrs Geyser
   And doesn't she look pretty sick ?
I'll bet it's because Mona Lisa
   Was hit on the hock with a brick.

Miss Blewitt says Monica threw it,
   But Monica says it was Joan,
And Joan's very thick with Miss Blewitt,
   So Monica's sulking alone.

And Margaret failed in her paces,
   Her withers got tied in a noose
So her coronets caught in the traces
   And now all her fetlocks are loose.

Oh, it's me now. I'm terribly nervous.
    I wonder if Smudges will shy.
She's practically certain to swerve as
    Her Pelham is over one eye.

Oh wasn't it naughty of Smudges ?
    Oh, Mummy, I'm sick with disgust.
She threw me in front of the Judges,
    And my silly old collarbone's bust.

John Betjeman

The Two Exquisites

Master Magnet and Miss Needle,
  When they met upon the road,
Were as nice a looking couple
  As you'd wish to see abroad.
Master Magnet and Miss Needle
  Soon to greet each other ran;
She was true as steel, and Magnet
  Was a most attractive man.

Robert Barnabas Brough

Chocolates

Here the seats are; George, old man,
Get some chocolates while you can.
Quick, the curtain's going to rise
(Either Bradbury's or Spry's).
'*The Castle ramparts, Elsinore*'
(That's not sufficient, get some more).
There's the *Ghost*: he does look wan
(Help yourself, and pass them on).
Doesn't *Hamlet* do it well?
(This one is a caramel).
Polonius's beard is fine
(Don't you grab; that big one's mine).
Look, the *King* can't bear the play
(Throw that squashy one away).
Now the *King* is at his prayers
(Splendid, there are two more layers).
Hamlet's going for his mother
(Come on, Tony, have another).
Poor *Ophelia*! Look, she's mad
(However many's Betty had?)
The *Queen* is dead, and so's the *King*
(Keep that lovely silver string).
Now even *Hamlet* can no more
(Pig! You've dropped it on the floor).
That last Act's simply full of shocks
(There's several left, so bring the box).

Guy Boas

Lynn

There was a young lady of Lynn
Who was born so uncommonly thin
    That when she essayed
    To drink lemonade,
She slipped through the straw and fell in.

                    Anonymous

The Yak

For hours the princess would not play or sleep
    Or take the air;
Her red mouth wore a look it meant to keep
    Unmelted there;
(Each tired courtier longed to shriek, or weep,
    But did not dare.)

Then one young duchess said: 'I'll to the King,
    And short and flat
I'll say, "Her Highness will not play or sing
    Or pet the cat;
Or feed the peacocks, or do anything –
    And that is that."'

So to the King she went, curtsied, and said,
    (No whit confused):
'Your Majesty, I would go home! The court is dead.
    Have me excused;
The little princess still declines,' – she tossed her head –
    'To be amused.'

Then to the princess stalked the King: 'What ho!' he roared,
    'What may you lack?
Why do you look, my love, so dull and bored
    With all this pack
Of minions?' She answered, while he waved his sword:
    'I want a yak.'

'A yak!' he cried (each courtier cried 'Yak! Yak!'
    As at a blow)
'Is that a figure on the zodiac?
    Or horse? Or crow?'
The princess sadly said to him: 'Alack
    I do not know.'

'We'll send the vassals far and wide, my dear!'
    Then quoth the King:
'They'll make a hunt for it, then come back here
    And bring the thing; –
But warily, – lest it be wild, or queer,
    Or have a sting.'

So off the vassals went, and well they sought
  On every track,
Till by and by in old Tibet they bought
  An ancient yak.
Yet when the princess saw it, she said naught
  But: 'Take it back!'

And what the courtiers thought they did not say
  (Save soft and low)
For that is surely far the wisest way
  As we all know;
While for the princess ? She went back to play!
          Tra-rill-a-la-lo!
          Tra-rill-a-la-lo!
          Tra-rill-a-la-lo!

Virna Sheard

The Two Kings

King David and King Solomon
  Led merry, merry lives,
With many, many lady friends
  And many, many wives;
But when old age crept over them,
  With many, many qualms,
King Solomon wrote the Proverbs
  And King David wrote the Psalms.

James Ball Naylor

The Common Cormorant

The common cormorant or shag
Lays eggs inside a paper bag
The reason you will see no doubt
It is to keep the lightning out
But what these unobservant birds
Have never noticed is that herds
Of wandering bears may come with buns
And steal the bags to hold the crumbs.

Anonymous

There was an old woman

There was an old woman who swallowed a fly;
I wonder why
She swallowed a fly.
Poor old woman, she's sure to die.

There was an old woman who swallowed a spider
That wriggled and jiggled and wriggled inside her.
She swallowed the spider to catch the fly,
I wonder why
She swallowed a fly.
Poor old woman, she's sure to die.

There was an old woman who swallowed a bird;
How absurd
To swallow a bird.
She swallowed the bird to catch the spider,
That wriggled and jiggled and wriggled inside her.
She swallowed the spider to catch the fly,
I wonder why
She swallowed a fly.
Poor old woman, she's sure to die.

There was an old woman who swallowed a cat;
Fancy that!
She swallowed a cat;
She swallowed the cat to catch the bird,
She swallowed the bird to catch the spider,
That wriggled and jiggled and wriggled inside her.
She swallowed the spider to catch the fly,
I wonder why
She swallowed a fly.
Poor old woman, she's sure to die.

There was an old woman who swallowed a dog;
She went the whole hog
And swallowed a dog;
She swallowed the dog to catch the cat,
She swallowed the cat to catch the bird,
She swallowed the bird to catch the spider,
That wriggled and jiggled and wriggled inside her.

She swallowed the spider to catch the fly,
I wonder why
She swallowed a fly.
Poor old woman, she's sure to die.

There was an old woman who swallowed a cow;
I wonder how
She swallowed a cow;
She swallowed the cow to catch the dog,
She swallowed the dog to catch the cat,
She swallowed the cat to catch the bird,
She swallowed the bird to catch the spider,
That wriggled and jiggled and wriggled inside her.
She swallowed the spider to catch the fly,
I wonder why
She swallowed a fly.
Poor old woman, she's sure to die.

There was an old woman who swallowed a horse;
She died of course!

Anonymous

The Reverend Sabine Baring-Gould

The Reverend Sabine Baring-Gould,
    Rector (sometime) at Lew,
Once at a Christmas party asked,
    'Whose pretty child are you ?'

(The Rector's family was long,
    His memory was poor,
And as to who was who had grown
    Increasingly unsure).

At this, the infant on the stair
    Most sorrowfully sighed.
'Whose pretty little girl am I ?
    Why, *yours*, papa !' she cried.

Charles Causley

The Elephant

Aunt Mary is my aunt,
  She took me to the Zoo.
She offered to the Elephant
  One bun – it wanted two.

Aunt Mary had a hat
  All cherries on her head.
The beast thought, 'Buns are good, but that
  Will do quite well instead.'

The creature smiled serene,
  And made a little bow.....
Aunt Mary's never, never seen
  Her hat from then till now.

Aunt Mary danced a jig,
  And wept till she was blind,
And screamed, 'You bad, old, ugly pig!'
  But, it didn't seem to mind.

John Joy Bell

The Ichthyosaurus

This poor beast found a doleful end –
  It makes me weep to tell it –
One day it overheard its name,
And then it pined and died of shame
  Because it could not spell it.

John Joy Bell

Logic

I have a copper penny and another copper penny,
  Well, then, of course, I have two copper pence;
I have a cousin Jenny and another cousin Jenny,
  Well, pray, then, do I have two cousin Jence?

Anonymous

146

The Song of the Camel

'Canary-birds feed on sugar and seed,
   Parrots have crackers to crunch;
And, as for the poodles, they tell me the noodles
   Have chickens and cream for their lunch.
      But there's never a question
      About MY digestion –
   ANYTHING does for me!

'Cats, you're aware, can repose in a chair,
   Chickens can roost upon rails;
Puppies are able to sleep in a stable,
   And oysters can slumber in pails.
      But no one supposes
      A poor Camel dozes –
   ANY PLACE does for me!

'Lambs are inclosed where it's never exposed,
   Coops are constructed for hens;
Kittens are treated to houses well heated,
   And pigs are protected by pens.
      But a Camel comes handy
      Wherever it's sandy –
   ANYWHERE does for me!

'People would laugh if you rode a giraffe,
   Or mounted the back of an ox;
It's nobody's habit to ride on a rabbit,
   Or try to bestraddle a fox.
      But as for a Camel, he's
      Ridden by families –
   ANY LOAD does for me!

'A snake is as round as a hole in the ground,
   And weasels are wavy and sleek;
And no alligator could ever be straighter
   Than lizards that live in a creek.
      But a Camel's all lumpy
      And bumpy and humpy –
   ANY SHAPE does for me!'

Charles Edward Carryl

The Knights

Two knights did once resolve to fight
   Upon an open plain,
And 'twas agreed no peace should be
   Till one of them was slain.
'Twas hard to say which of the two
   The best man should be reckoned,
For both their heads, most strange to view,
   Flew off at the selfsame second.
Now, some maintain this one was best,
   And some assert 'twas t'other;
It lay between them, and I think,
   If not one, 'twas the other.

Charles Henry Ross

Gasbags

I'm thankful that the sun and moon
Are both hung up so high
That no pretentious hand can stretch
And pull them from the sky.
If they were not, I have no doubt,
But some reforming ass
Would recommend to take them down
And light the world with gas.

Anonymous

Going to The Dogs

My granddad, viewing earth's worn cogs,
Said things were going to the dogs;
His granddad in his house of logs,
Said things were going to the dogs;
His granddad in the Flemish bogs,
Said things were going to the dogs;
His granddad in his old skin togs,
Said things were going to the dogs;
There's one thing that I have to state –
The dogs have had a good long wait.

Anonymous

You are old, Father William

'You are old, Father William,' the young man said,
  'And your hair has become very white;
And yet you incessantly stand on your head –
  Do you think, at your age, it is right ?'

'In my youth,' Father William replied to his son,
  'I feared it might injure the brain;
But, now that I'm perfectly sure I have none,
  Why, I do it again and again.'

'You are old,' said the youth, 'as I mentioned before,
  And have grown most uncommonly fat;
Yet you turned a back-somersault in at the door –
  Pray, what is the reason for that ?'

'In my youth,' said the sage, as he shook his grey locks,
  'I kept all my limbs very supple
By the use of this ointment – one shilling the box –
  Allow me to sell you a couple ?'

'You are old,' said the youth, 'and your jaws are too weak
  For anything tougher than suet;
Yet you finished the goose, with the bones and the beak –
  Pray, how did you manage to do it ?'

'In my youth,' said his father, 'I took to the law,
  And argued each case with my wife;
And the muscular strength, which it gave to my jaw,
  Has lasted the rest of my life.'

'You are old,' said the youth, 'one would hardly suppose
  That your eye was as steady as ever;
Yet you balanced an eel on the end of your nose –
  What made you so awfully clever ?'

'I have answered three questions, and that is enough,'
  Said his father. 'Don't give yourself airs!
Do you think I can listen all day to such stuff ?
  Be off, or I'll kick you downstairs!'

                                        Lewis Carroll

Farewell

Farewell, my friends – farewell and hail!
I'm off to seek the Holy Grail.
    I cannot tell you why.
Remember, please, when I am gone,
'Twas Aspiration led me on.
Tiddlely-widdlely tootle-oo,
All I want is to stay with you,
    But here I go. Goodbye.

Clarence Day

W. C. Field's Epitaph

Pure Happiness

A fair little girl sat under a tree,
Sewing as long as her eyes could see;
Then smoothed her work, and folded it right,
And said, 'Dear work! Good Night! Good Night!'

Richard Monckton Milnes

Notes and Acknowledgements

I compiled this book by reading through other books, most of whose titles are listed below (page 154). Though I already knew some of the poems reprinted, several of the Anthologists Consulted, William Cole, J. M. Cohen, Iona and Peter Opie, for example, introduced me to authors and to poems I had no knowledge of. My debt to their diligence and to their taste is considerable.

It is my pleasure to thank the following Librarians for the patience and the kindness they have shown me in my search for out-of-the-way books, and for their generosity in suggesting titles I should otherwise have missed: Mr Douglas Matthews and the Staff of the London Library; Mr Jonathan Barker of the Arts Council Library; Mrs Doris Aubrey and the Staff of the West Hill District Library, London Borough of Wandsworth; Mr Lionel Baker and the Staff of the Victoria Library, London Borough of Westminster; Mr H. J. Vincent and the Staff of the Bancroft Road Library, London Borough of Tower Hamlets; the Staff of Australia House Reference Library; the Staff of the Reading Room, Department of Printed Books, the British Library; and to Mr Robert Vas Dias, then General Secretary of the Poetry Society.

May I also thank Miss Annabel Bartlett, Mr Samuel Carr, Mr Peter Clarke, Dr Germaine Greer, Lady Cristian Hesketh, Mr Tony Rushton, Mr Alan Sillitoe, Miss Ruth Taylor and Miss Laura Warner for their advice and encouragement.

Every effort has been made to discover the owners of copyright material reprinted. On receiving notification, any omissions that have occurred will be rectified.

Authors and Sources

ANONYMOUS: Most of the poems reprinted over this title, particularly the Epigrams, Epitaphs, and Limericks, are traditional and will be found in one or other of the Anthologies Consulted; quite often they appear in several versions, in which case I have chosen the text I preferred. I have not dated these poems but very few of them are pre-1800 and the majority seem to have been written between 1860 and 1930.

George Barker
My Sister Clarissa spits twice if I kiss her — Reprinted by permission of Faber and Faber Ltd from *To Aylsham Fair* by George Barker

Hilaire Belloc
The Hippopotamus
The Frog
Matilda — Reprinted by permission of Gerald Duckworth and Company Ltd from *Cautionary Verses* (Duckworth 1976 12th imp)

E. C. Bentley
Sir Christopher Wren — Reprinted by permission of Nicolas Bentley from *Clerihews Complete* by E. C. Bentley (Werner Laurie, 1951)

John Betjeman
Hunter Trials — Reprinted by permission of John Murray (Publishers) Ltd from *John Betjeman Collected Poems*

Charles Causley
The Reverend Sabine Baring-Gould — Reprinted by permission of David Higham Associates Ltd from *Charles Causley Collected Poems* (Macmillan)

A. E. Housman
Amelia — Reprinted by permission of The Society of Authors as the literary representative of the Estate of A. E. Housman; and Jonathan Cape Ltd, publishers of A. E. Housman's *Collected Poems*

Felicia Lamport
→*Drawn Onward*← — Reprinted by permission of the author and publisher from *Cultural Slag* by Felicia Lamport (Victor Gollancz Ltd, 1966)

E. V. Lucas
The Welsh — Reprinted by permission of Associated Book Publishers Ltd from *Playtime and Company* by E. V. Lucas (Methuen & Co Ltd)

Max Miller
Mary had a Little Bear — Reprinted by permission of Robson Books Ltd from *The Max Miller Blue Book*, compiled by Barry Took

Spike Milligan
The ABC — From *The Little Pot Boiler*
Ancient Chinese Song — From *A Book of Bits*, both by Spike Milligan.
Holy Smoke — Reprinted by permission of Dennis Dobson Publishers

A. A. Milne
Miss James — Reprinted by permission of Associated Book Publishers Ltd from *When We Were Young* by A. A. Milne (Methuen Children's Books Ltd)

Ogden Nash
The Duck
The Pig — Reprinted by permission of the Estate of the Late Ogden Nash

Shaw Neilson
A Brilliant Idea — Reprinted by permission of Mrs Margot Ludowici

Alfred Noyes
The Man Who Discovered the Use of a Chair — Reprinted by permission of John Murray (Publishers) Ltd from *Alfred Noyes Collected Poems* (1950)

Carol Paine
School Report — Reprinted by permission of *Punch*

Mervyn Peake
Of Pygmies, Palms and Pirates — Reprinted by permission of Peter Owen, London from *Book of Nonsense* by Mervyn Peake (1972)

William Plomer
Ecstasy (Part V of The Naiad of Ostend: or, A Fatal Passion) — Reprinted by permission of the Estate of William Plomer from *William Plomer Collected Poems* (Jonathan Cape, 1960)

Laura E. Richards
Polar Bear's Party — Reprinted by permission of Little, Brown and

Eletelephony	Company, from *Tirra Lirra* by Laura E. Richards (1932)
Margery Maggot	Reprinted by permission of Trustee u/w Laura
Prudence Pedantic	E. Richards
Woffsky-Poffsky	
After a Visit to the Natural History Museum	
Ethel Talbot Scheffauer	
A Reply from the Akond of Swat	Reprinted by permission of the *New Statesman*
Virna Sheard	
The Yak	Reprinted by permission of Terence Sheard from *Leaves in the Wind* (Ryerson Press Ltd)
Stevie Smith	
Croft	Reprinted by permission of James MacGibbon, the executor, from *Stevie Smith Collected Poems* (Allen Lane)
Elizabeth Wordsworth	
The Good and the Clever	Reprinted by permission of the Longman Group Ltd from *St Christopher and Other Poems* by Elizabeth Wordsworth
Ronald Young	
The Zebra	Reprinted by permission of Maurice O'Connell from *The Book of Humorous Verse* by Carolyn Wells (Doubleday, Doran and Co)

Other Anthologists and Anthologies consulted

Adams, W. Davenport, The Comic Poets of the Nineteenth Century 1864(?)
— English Epigrams 1878
— Song of Society 1880
Alington, Cyril, Poets at Play 1942
Auden, W. H., The Faber Book of Modern American Verse 1956
Barr, James, American Humorous Verse 1891
Beable, W. H., Epitaphs 1925
Britton, James, The Oxford Book of Verse for Juniors 1957
Caine, W. R. H., Humorous Poems of the Century 1889
Cohen, J. M., Comic and Curious Verse 1961
— More Comic and Curious Verse 1964
— Yet More Comic and Curious Verse 1969
Cole, William, The Birds and the Beasts Were There 1963
— The Fireside Book of Humorous Poetry 1965

— Oh, What Nonsense! 1966
— Beastly Boys and Ghastly Girls 1970
— Oh, How Silly! 1971
Cook, T. A., An Anthology of Humorous Verse 1902
Daly, T. A., A Little Book of American Humorous Verse 1927
Deane, Anthony C., A Little Book of Light Verse 1902
De La Mare, Walter, Come Hither 1928
Dobson, William T., Poetical Ingenuities 1882
Fairley, W., Epitaphiana 1875
Fyleman, Rose, Here We Come A'Piping 1936
Ginnette, Lillian, Light and Humorous Verse 1935
Green, Lancelyn, A Century of Humorous Verse 1959
— A Book of Nonsense n.d.
Grigson, Geoffrey, Unrespectable Verse 1971
Heap, P. H., Humorous Tales in Verse n.d.
Henderson, W., Victorian Street Ballads 1937
Hoke, Helen, The Family Book of Humour 1975
Hollowood, Bernard, Women in Punch 1961
Humorous Poems by English and American Writers 1880 (?)
Hunt, Leigh, Wit and Humour Selected from the English Poets 1846
Ingrams, Richard, The Works of J. B. Morton 1974
Ireson, Barbara, The Young Puffin Book of Verse 1970
Knox, E. R. V., Humorous Verse 1931
Laing, Allan M., Prayers and Graces 1944
Lamb, Charles and Mary, Poetry for Children 1808
Lehmann, Geoffrey, Comic Australian Verse 1972
Loaring, Henry James, Curious Records 1872
Locker-Lampson, F., Lyra Elegantiarum n.d.
Lynd, Sylvia, The Children's Omnibus 1932
McEachran, F., Spells 1953
Melville, H. and L., An Anthology of Humorous Verse 1910
Miall, S., Poets at Play 1932
Moorhouse, Reed, Burning Gold 1929
Morley, H., Playful Poems 1891
Nash, Ogden, The Moon is Shining Bright as Day 1953
Nimmo, William P., The Book of Humorous Poetry n.d.
Nonsense Omnibus, The, 1943
Norfolk, Edward Horatio, Gleanings in Graveyards 1861
O'Donoghue, J. D., The Humour of Ireland 1894
Opie, Peter and Iona, The Oxford Book of Children's Verse 1973
Parton, J., Humorous Poems 1881
Partridge, Eric, Comic Alphabets 1961
Pearson's Humorous Reciter and Reader 1904
Powell, G. H., Musa Jocosa 1894
Puzzler, The, A Collection of 200 Enigmas, Anagrams, and Conundrums n.d.
Reed, Gwendolyn, Out of the Ark 1968
Reed, Langton, Nonsense Verses 1925
— Complete Book of Limericks n.d.
Rhys, Ernest, A New Book of Sense and Nonsense 1928
Roberts, Dennis Kilham, Straw In the Hair 1938
Roberts, Michael, The Faber Book of Comic Verse 1942

Silcock, Arnold, Verse and Worse 1958
Slater, W. E., Humour In Verse 1937
Smith, Janet Adam, The Faber Book of Children's Verse 1953
Squire, Sir John, The Comic Muse n.d.
Stewart, Aubrey, English Epigrams and Epitaphs 1897
Took, Barry, The Max Miller Blue Book 1975
Vines, W. S., Whips and Scorpions 1932
Wanna, Bill, Robust, Ribald, and Rude Verse in Australia 1972
Watson, Julia, The Armada Lion Book of Young Verse 1973
Wells, Carolyn, The Book of Humorous Verse n.d.
Whitlock, Pamela, All Day Long 1954
Woods, R. L., A Treasury of the Familiar 1942
Wyndham-Lewis, D. B., The Nonsensibus 1936

Index of Authors

Index of First Lines